TABLE of CONTENTS

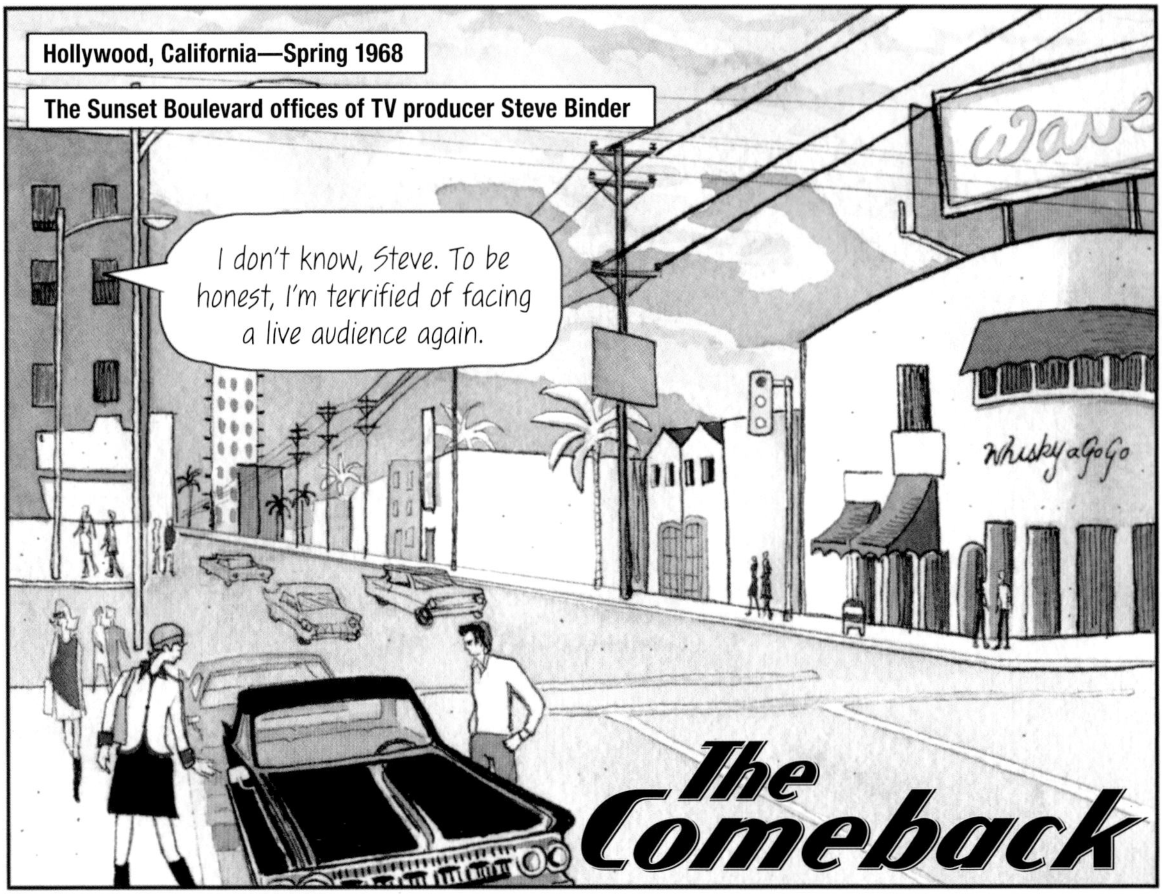
Hollywood, California—Spring 1968
The Sunset Boulevard offices of TV producer Steve Binder
I don't know, Steve. To be honest, I'm terrified of facing a live audience again.
Whisky a Go Go
The Comeback

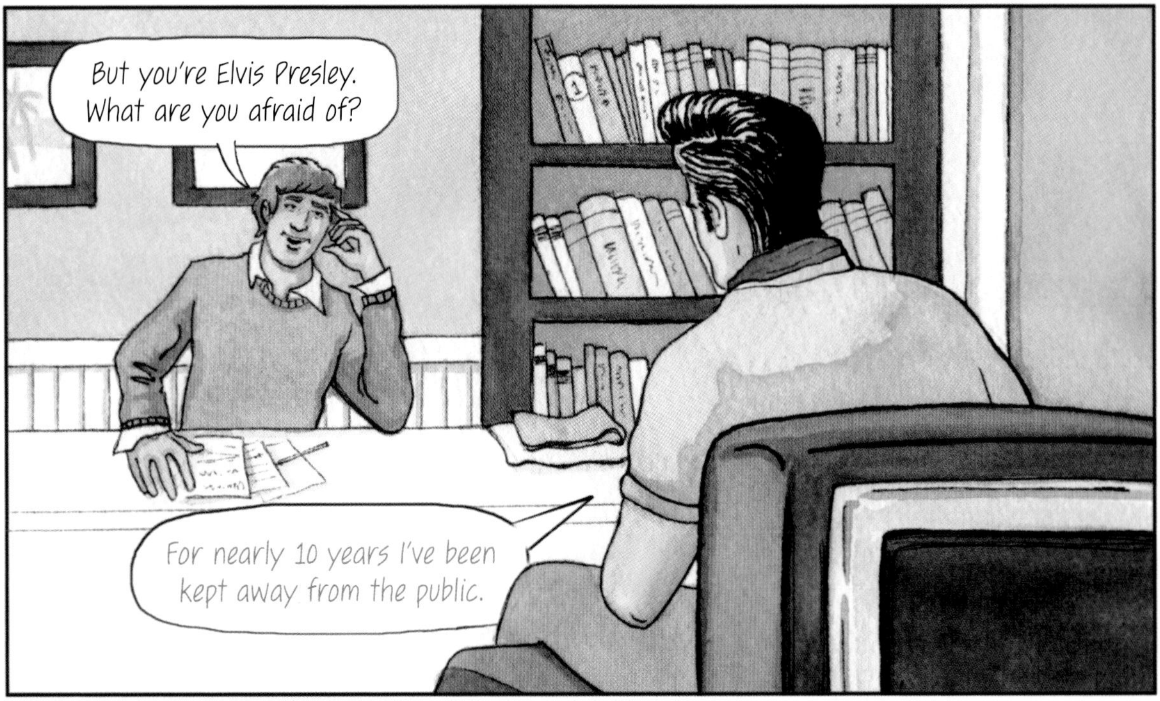
But you're Elvis Presley. What are you afraid of?
For nearly 10 years I've been kept away from the public.

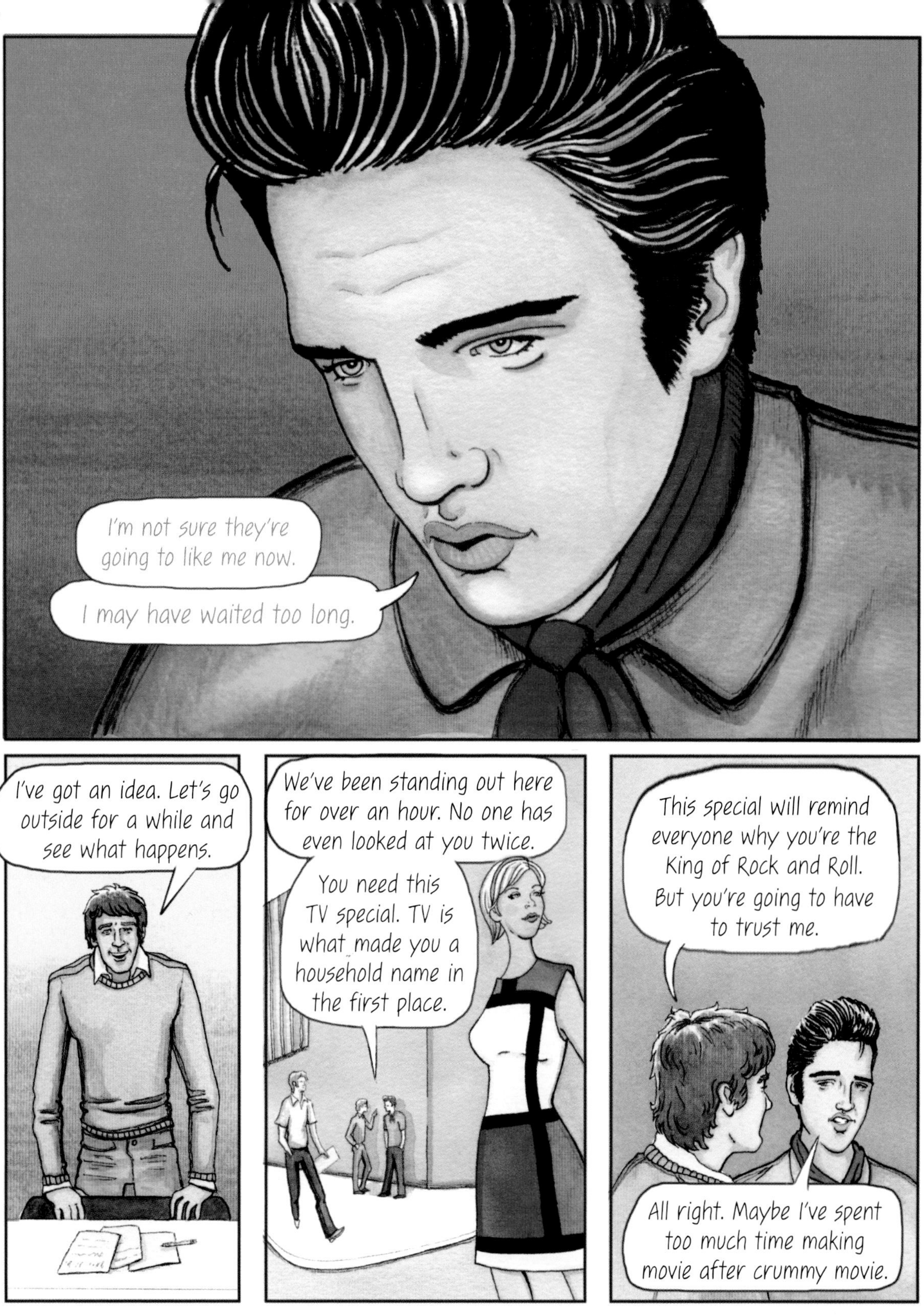
I'm not sure they're going to like me now.
I may have waited too long.
I've got an idea. Let's go outside for a while and see what happens.
We've been standing out here for over an hour. No one has even looked at you twice.
You need this TV special. TV is what made you a household name in the first place.
This special will remind everyone why you're the King of Rock and Roll. But you're going to have to trust me.
All right. Maybe I've spent too much time making movie after crummy movie.

At the Movies

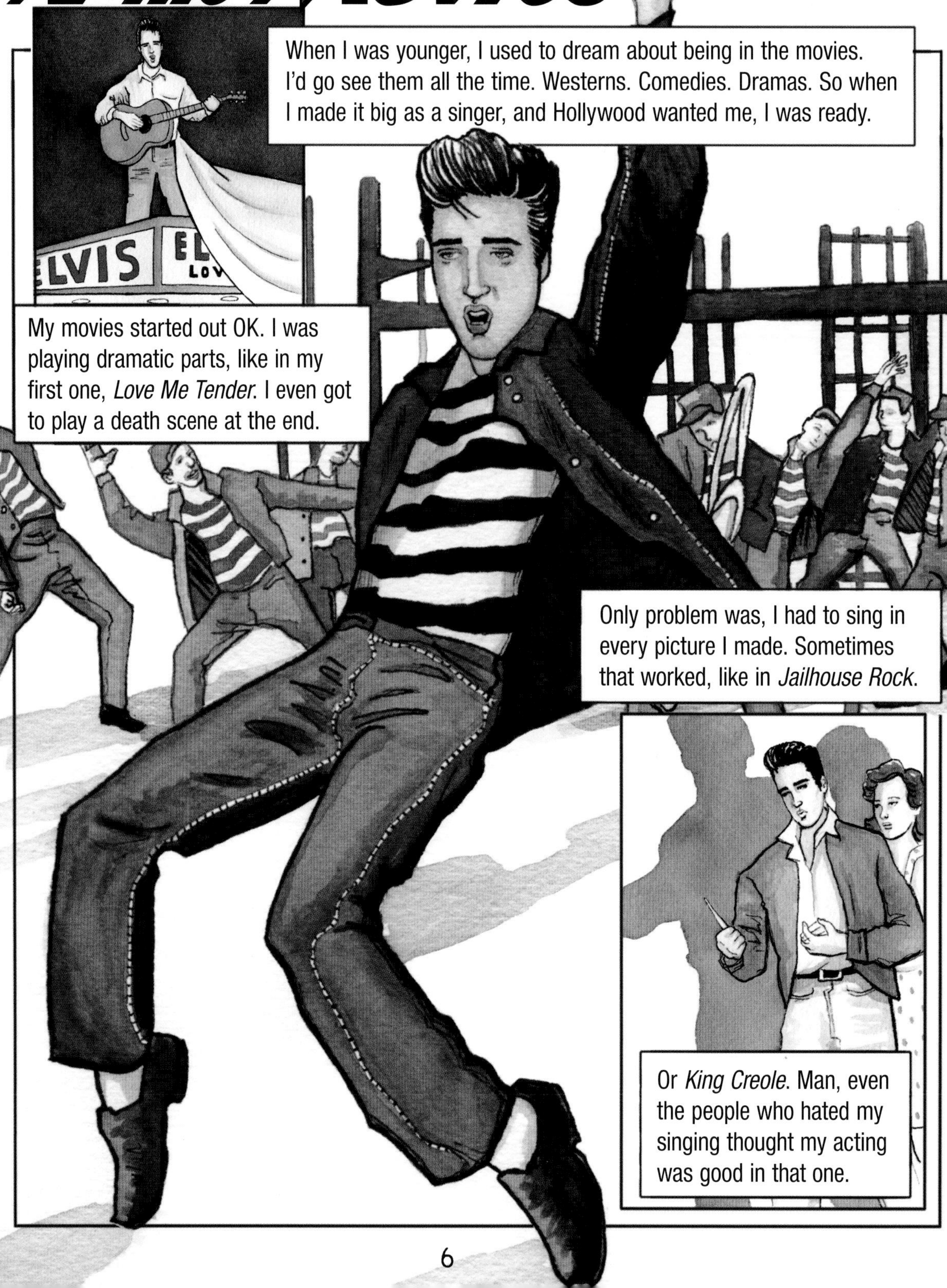

When I was younger, I used to dream about being in the movies. I'd go see them all the time. Westerns. Comedies. Dramas. So when I made it big as a singer, and Hollywood wanted me, I was ready.
ELVIS
My movies started out OK. I was playing dramatic parts, like in my first one, *Love Me Tender*. I even got to play a death scene at the end.
Only problem was, I had to sing in every picture I made. Sometimes that worked, like in *Jailhouse Rock*.
Or *King Creole*. Man, even the people who hated my singing thought my acting was good in that one.

I got back from serving in the military in 1960. Then I played a singing army sergeant in *G.I. Blues*.

Soon after that, the budgets for my movies got smaller, and the scripts got dumber. I was singing duets with myself in *Kissin' Cousins*.

Harum Scarum was real bad. My manager almost talked the producers into adding a talking camel for laughs.

And I don't know how many singing race car driver movies I've made.

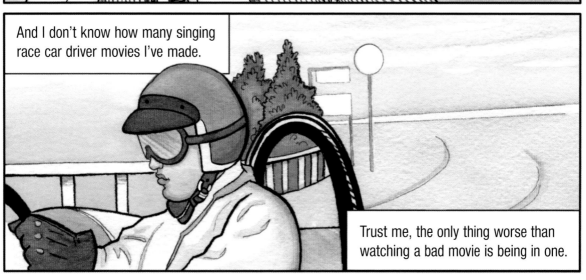

Trust me, the only thing worse than watching a bad movie is being in one.

If I Can Dream

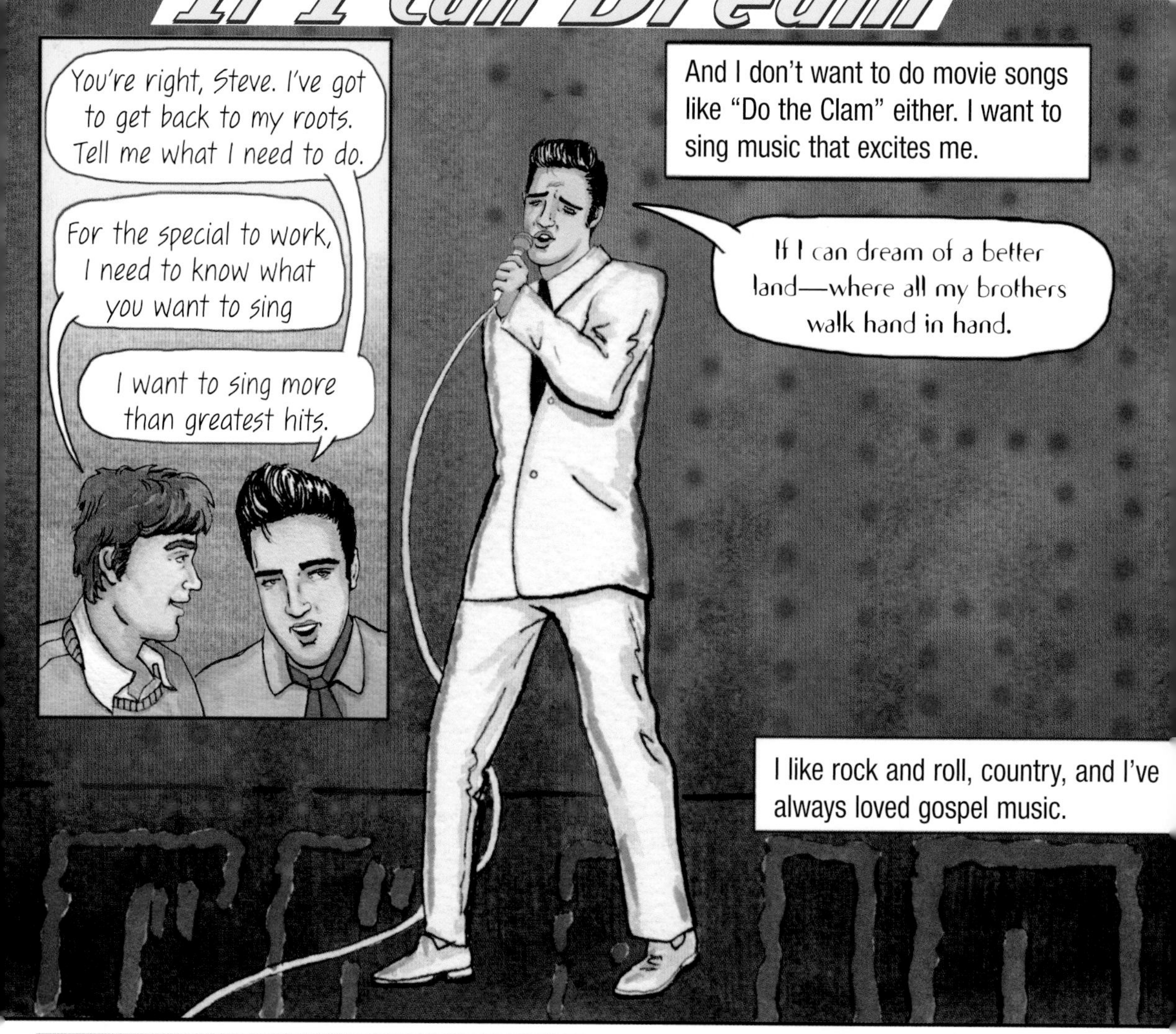

You're right, Steve. I've got to get back to my roots. Tell me what I need to do.
For the special to work, I need to know what you want to sing
I want to sing more than greatest hits.
And I don't want to do movie songs like "Do the Clam" either. I want to sing music that excites me.
If I can dream of a better land—where all my brothers walk hand in hand.
I like rock and roll, country, and I've always loved gospel music.

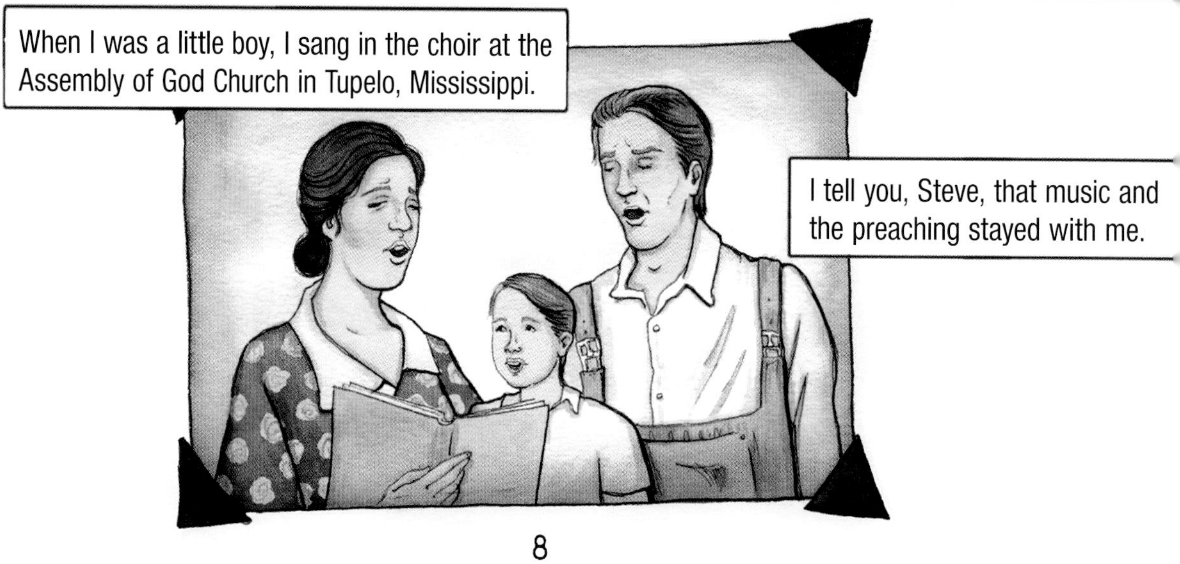

When I was a little boy, I sang in the choir at the Assembly of God Church in Tupelo, Mississippi.
I tell you, Steve, that music and the preaching stayed with me.

For awhile, I thought I might even become a preacher. But I knew there was a better way to share my feelings.

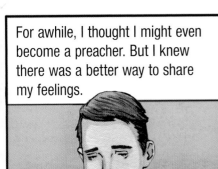

I was 10 years old when I entered a state fair talent contest. I was never nervous while singing in church, but this was different.

Old Shep, he has gone where the good doggies go.

I came in fifth place. I won $5 and free rides.

Steve, for this TV special I need a song that incorporates everything about me.

While I can dream, please let my dream come true ... right now!

I need a real showstopper.

What do you think of the song?

I love it. There's a real message of hope in those words.

But this was a closed set. Next, I have to get ready to sing for a live audience again.

Now or Never

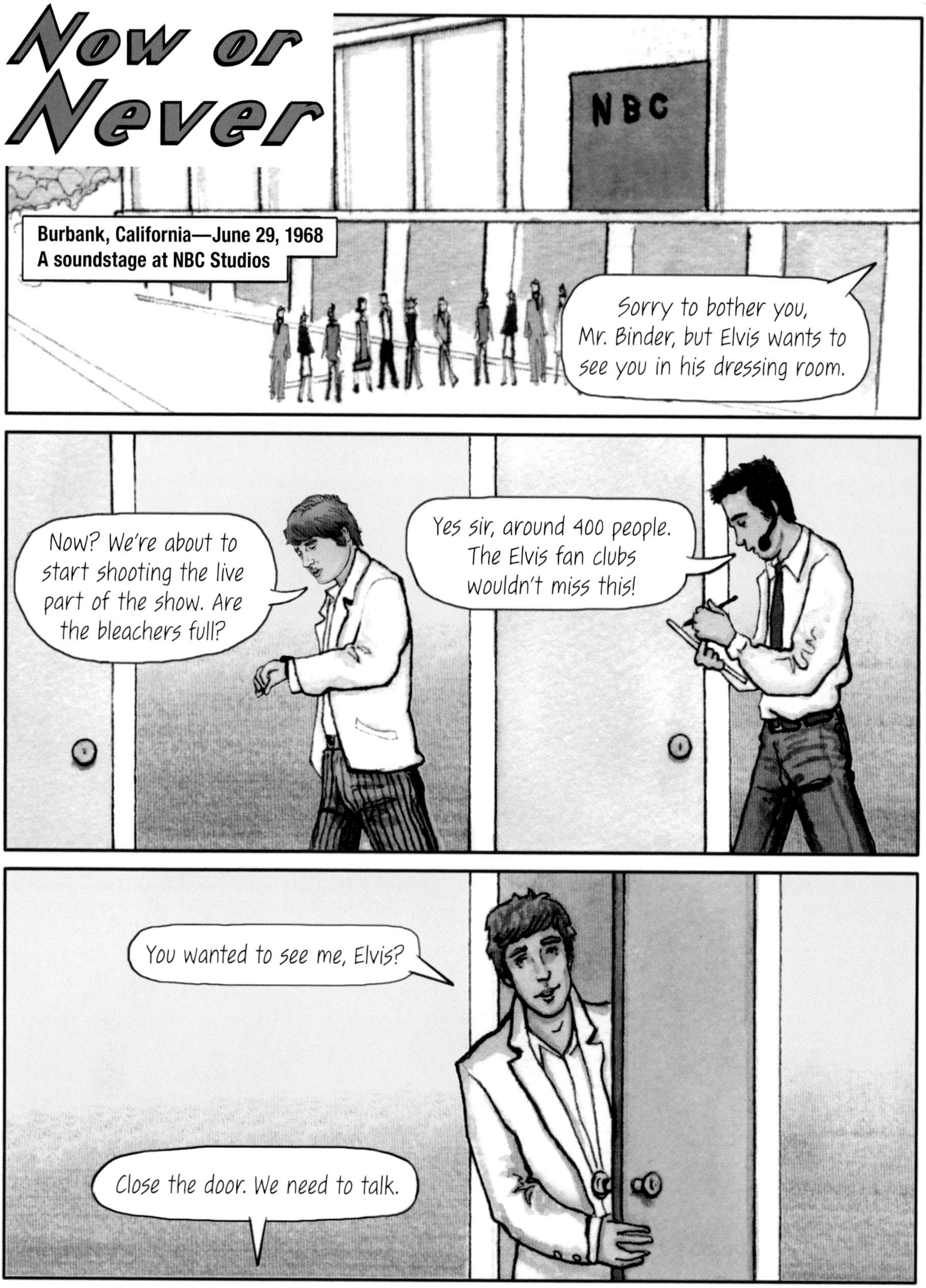

Burbank, California—June 29, 1968
A soundstage at NBC Studios
NBC
Sorry to bother you, Mr. Binder, but Elvis wants to see you in his dressing room.
Now? We're about to start shooting the live part of the show. Are the bleachers full?
Yes sir, around 400 people. The Elvis fan clubs wouldn't miss this!
You wanted to see me, Elvis?
Close the door. We need to talk.

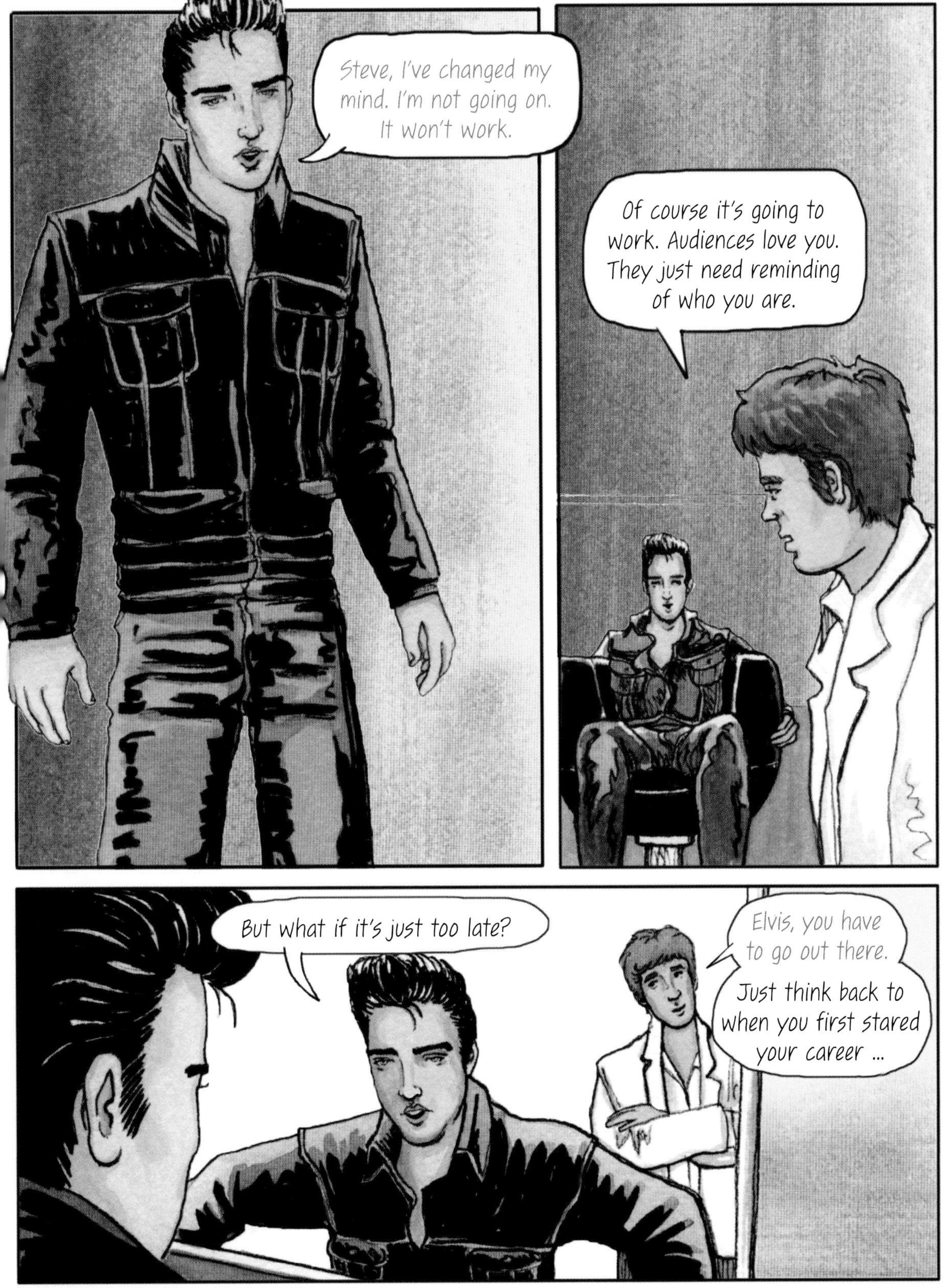
Steve, I've changed my mind. I'm not going on. It won't work.
Of course it's going to work. Audiences love you. They just need reminding of who you are.
But what if it's just too late?
Elvis, you have to go out there.
Just think back to when you first stared your career ...

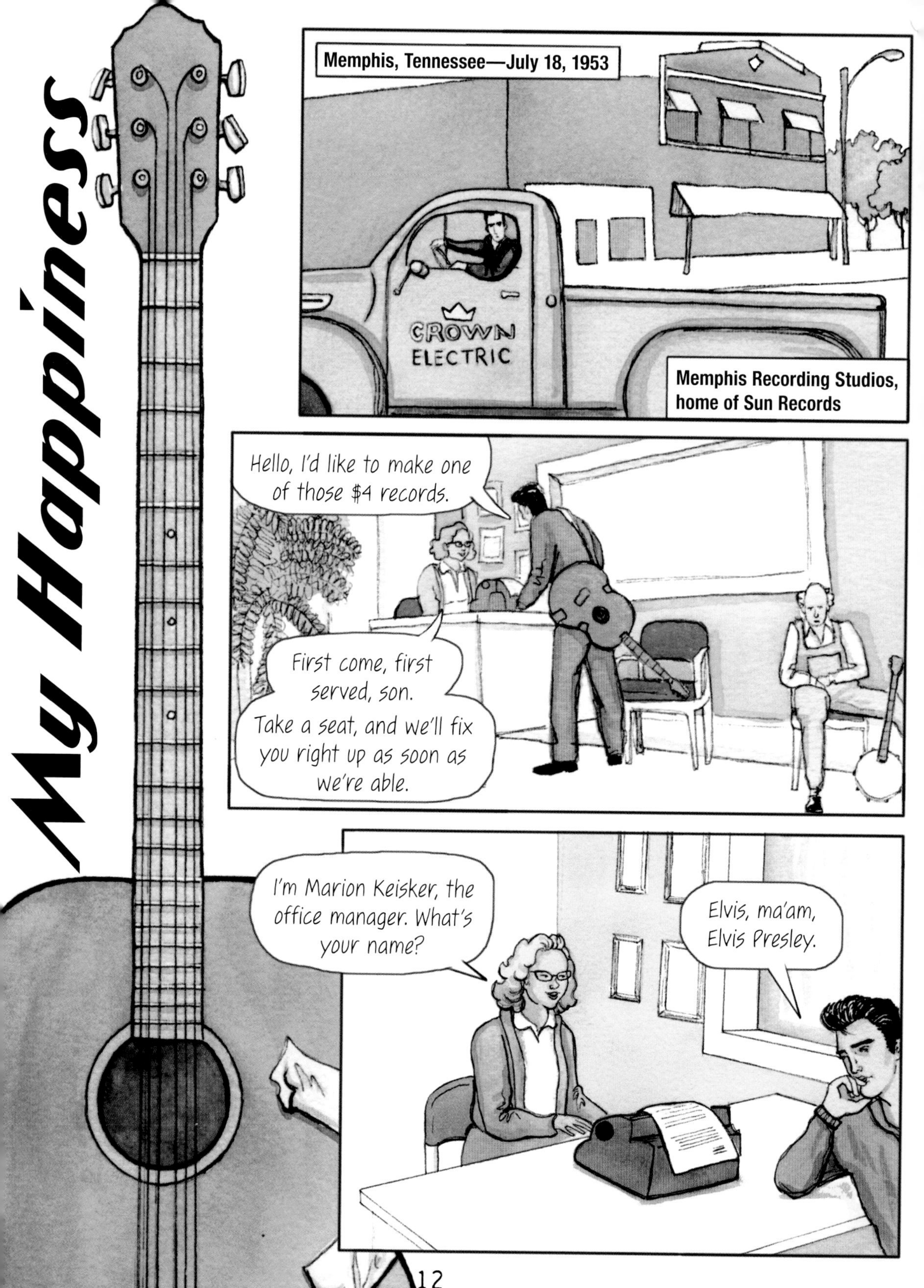
My Happiness
Memphis, Tennessee—July 18, 1953
CROWN ELECTRIC
Memphis Recording Studios, home of Sun Records
Hello, I'd like to make one of those $4 records.
First come, first served, son.
Take a seat, and we'll fix you right up as soon as we're able.
I'm Marion Keisker, the office manager. What's your name?
Elvis, ma'am, Elvis Presley.

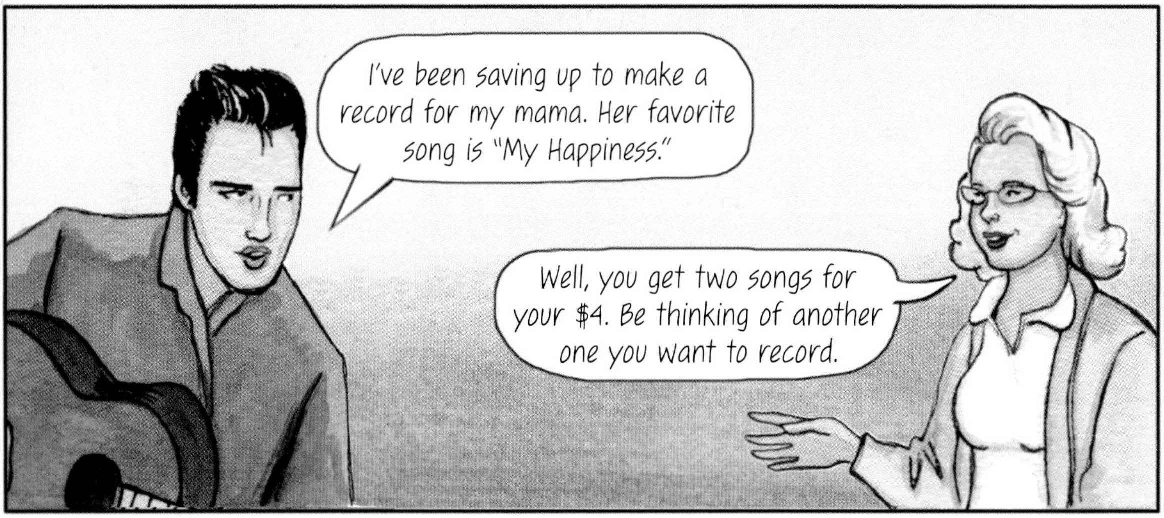
I've been saving up to make a record for my mama. Her favorite song is "My Happiness."
Well, you get two songs for your $4. Be thinking of another one you want to record.

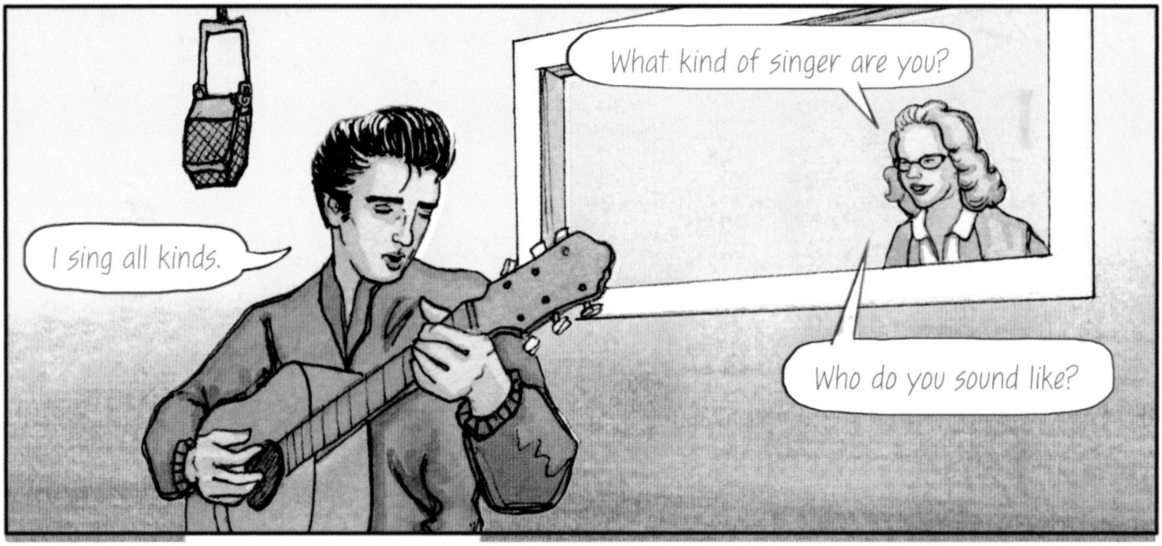
What kind of singer are you?
I sing all kinds.
Who do you sound like?

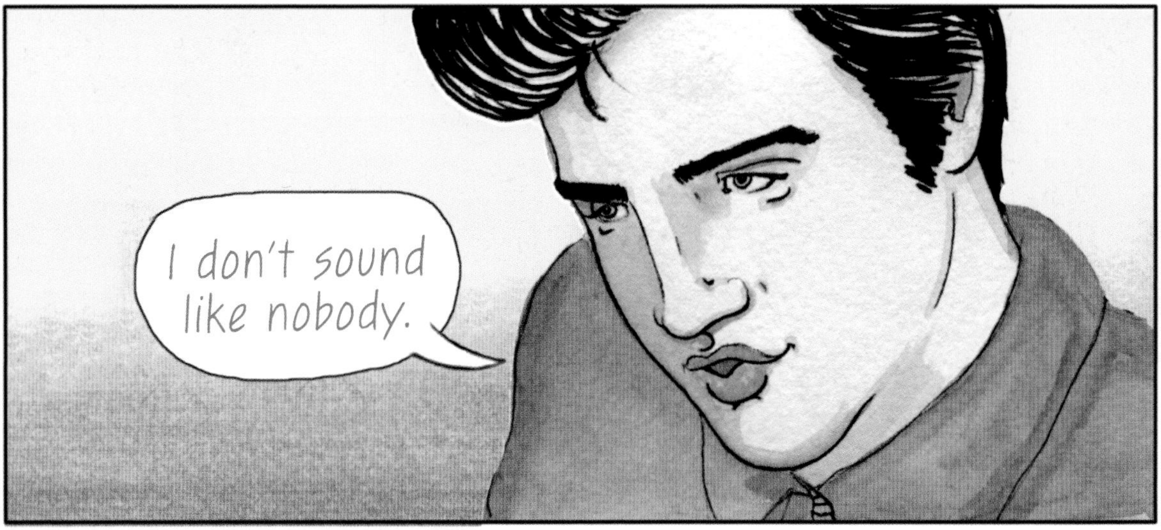
I don't sound like nobody.

Mr. Sam Phillips

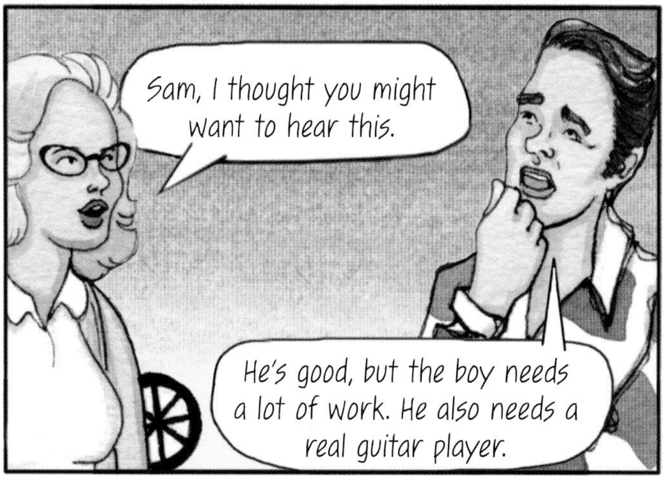
Sam, I thought you might want to hear this.
He's good, but the boy needs a lot of work. He also needs a real guitar player.

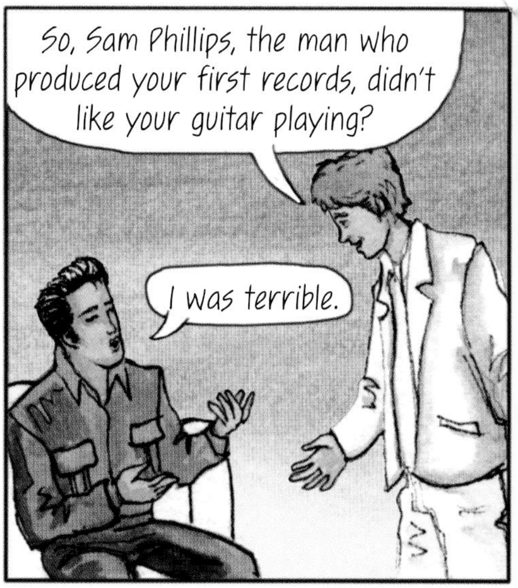
So, Sam Phillips, the man who produced your first records, didn't like your guitar playing?
I was terrible.

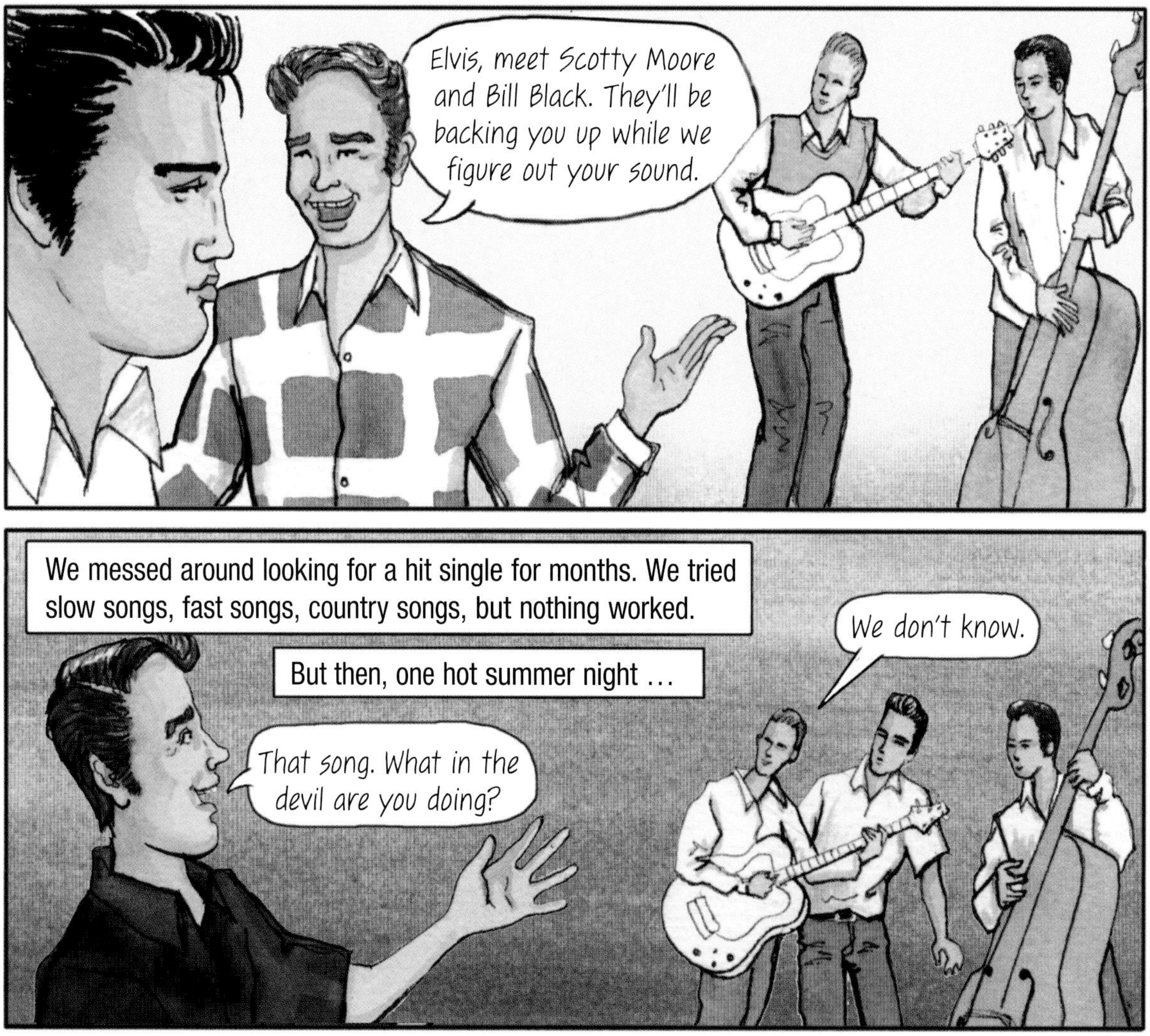
Elvis, meet Scotty Moore and Bill Black. They'll be backing you up while we figure out your sound.
We messed around looking for a hit single for months. We tried slow songs, fast songs, country songs, but nothing worked.
But then, one hot summer night …
That song. What in the devil are you doing?
We don't know.

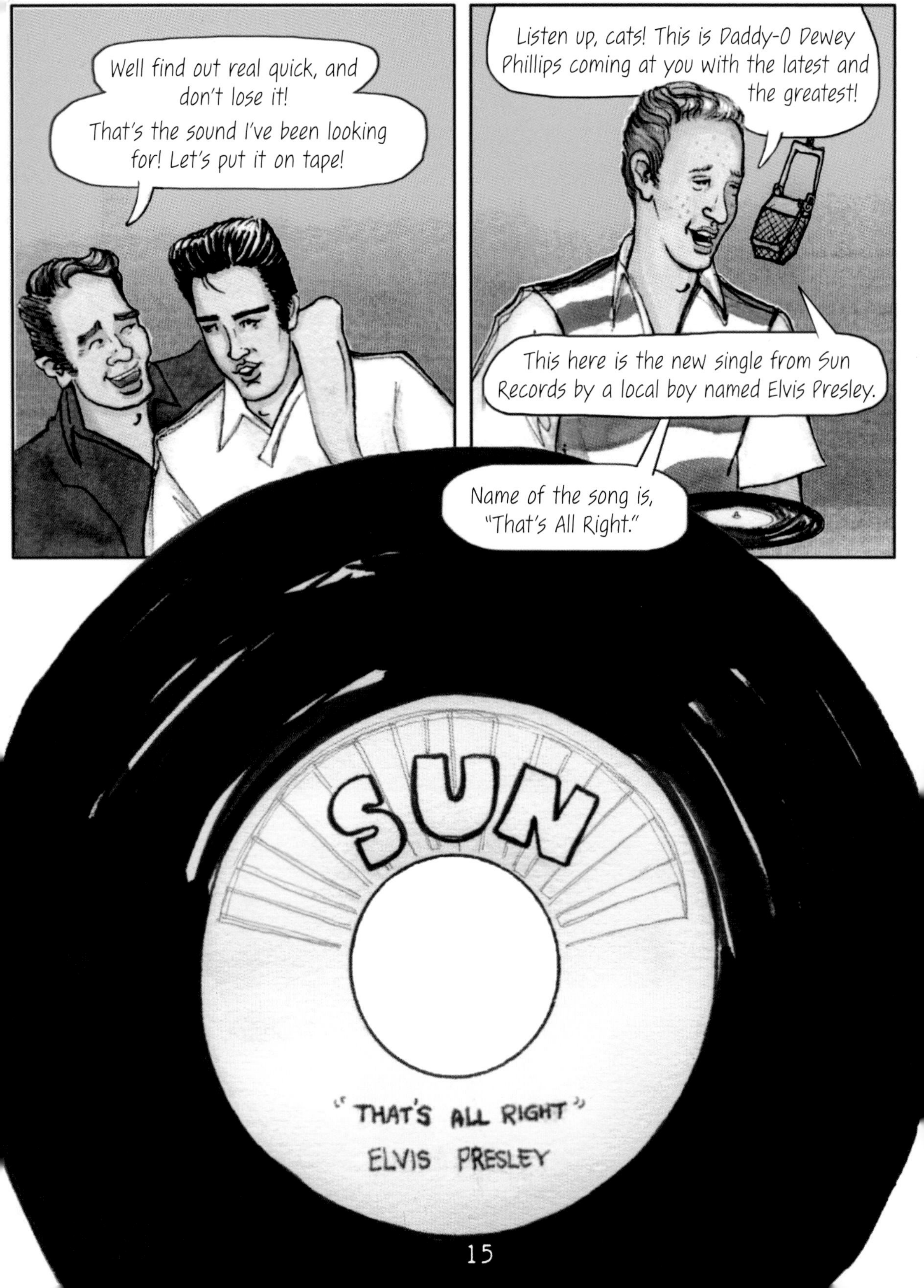
Well find out real quick, and don't lose it!
That's the sound I've been looking for! Let's put it on tape!
Listen up, cats! This is Daddy-O Dewey Phillips coming at you with the latest and the greatest!
This here is the new single from Sun Records by a local boy named Elvis Presley.
Name of the song is, "That's All Right."
SUN
"THAT'S ALL RIGHT"
ELVIS PRESLEY

Elvis on Tour

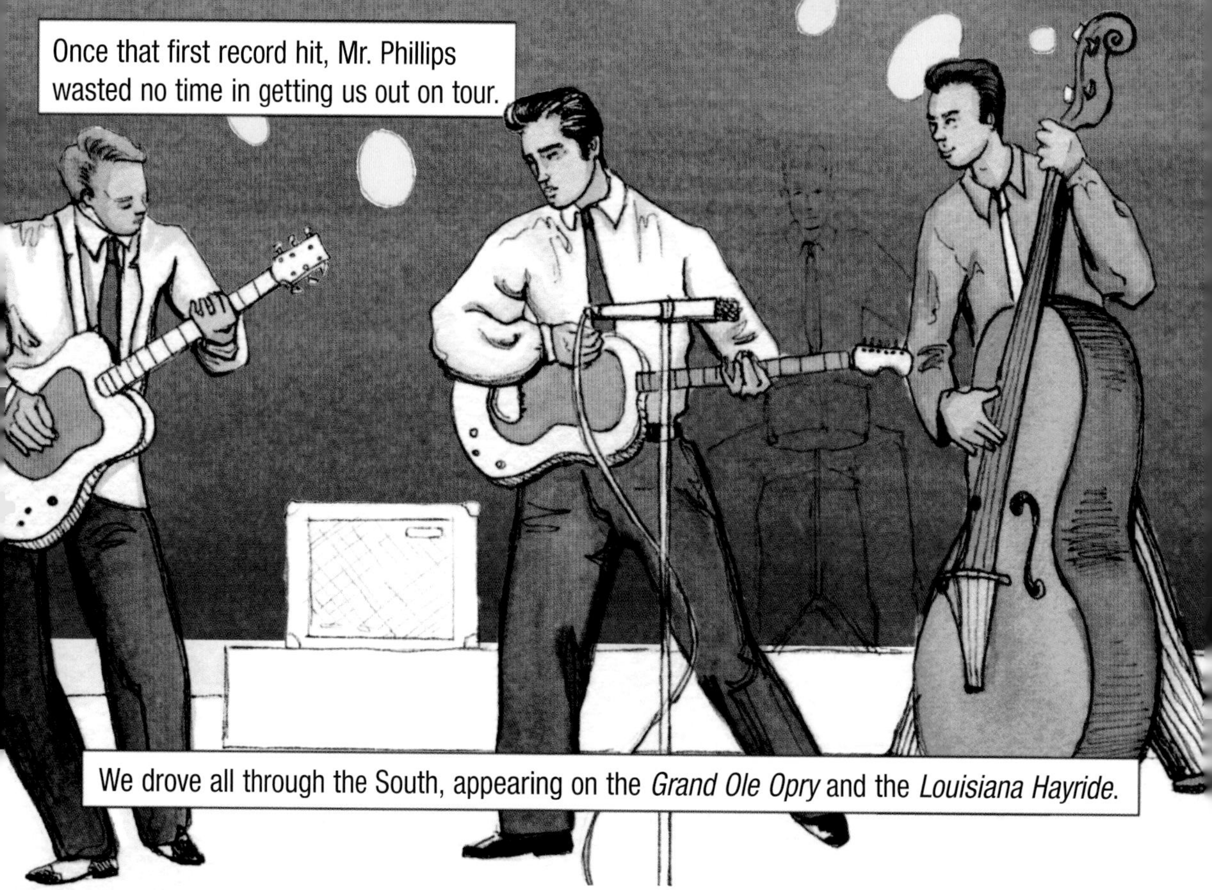
Once that first record hit, Mr. Phillips wasted no time in getting us out on tour.
We drove all through the South, appearing on the *Grand Ole Opry* and the *Louisiana Hayride*.

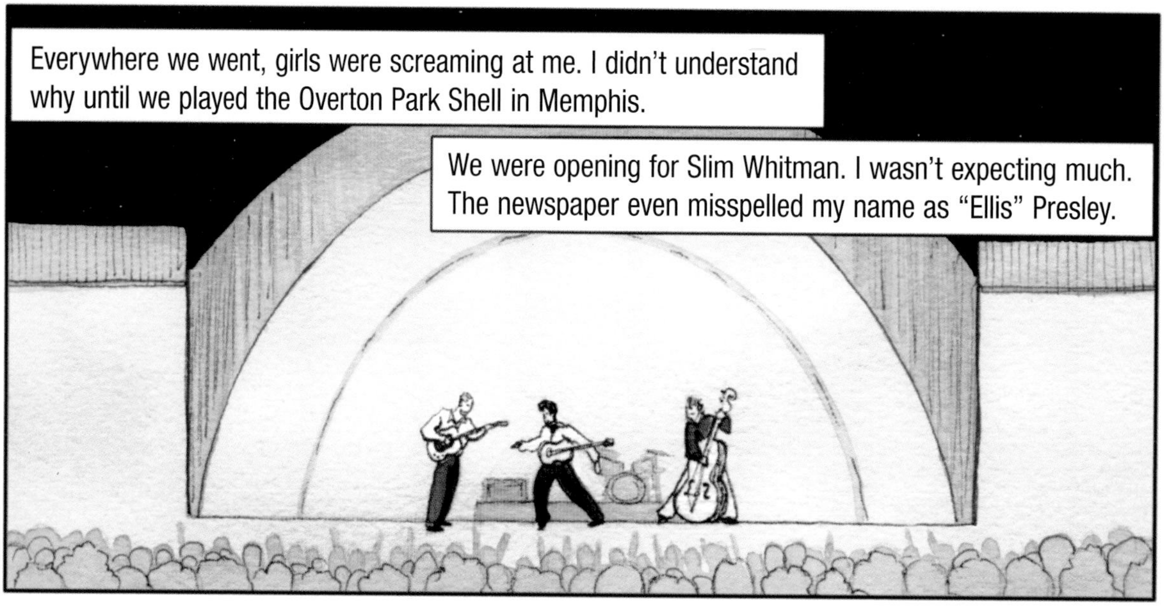
Everywhere we went, girls were screaming at me. I didn't understand why until we played the Overton Park Shell in Memphis.
We were opening for Slim Whitman. I wasn't expecting much. The newspaper even misspelled my name as "Ellis" Presley.

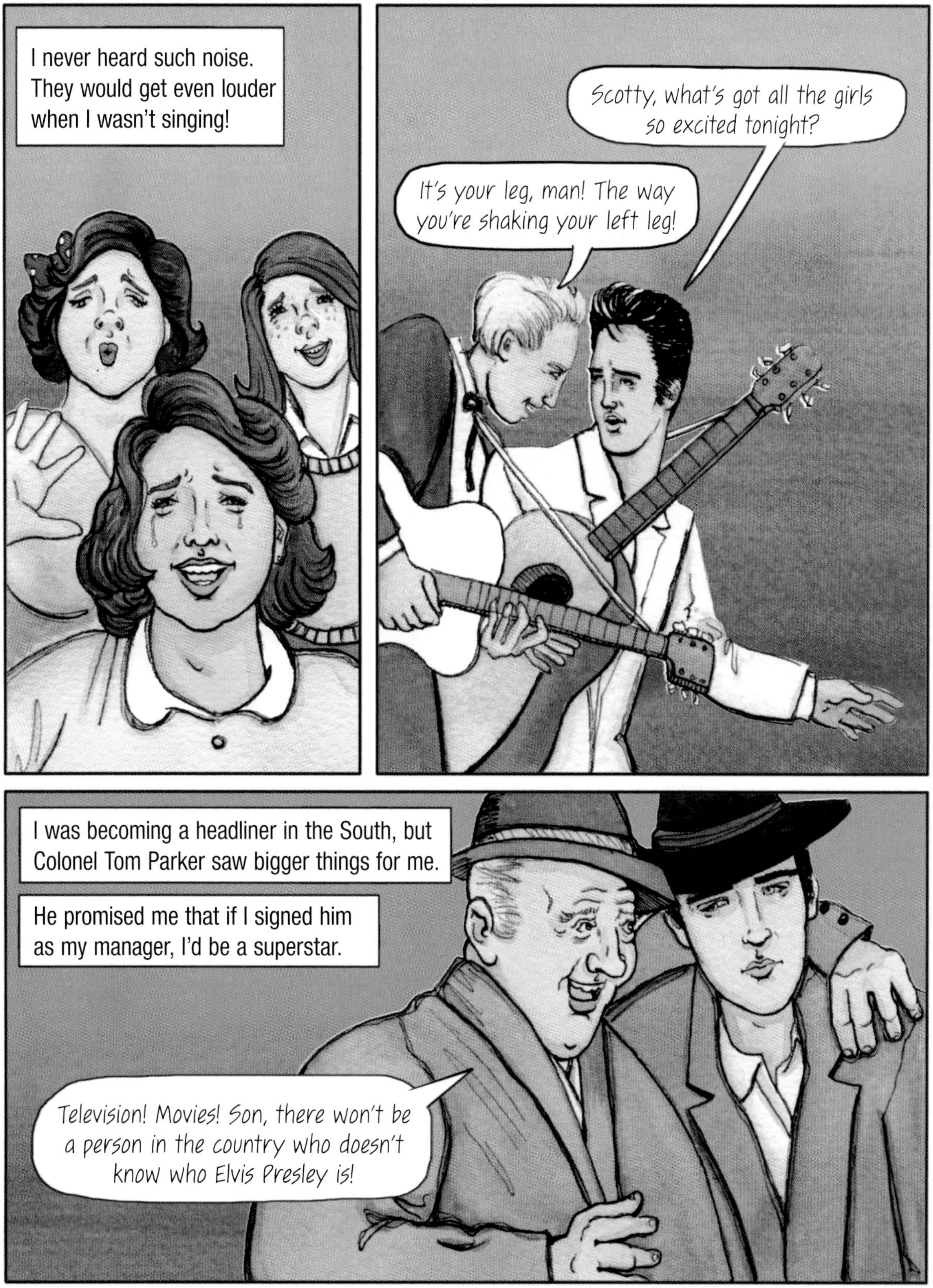
I never heard such noise. They would get even louder when I wasn't singing!
Scotty, what's got all the girls so excited tonight?
It's your leg, man! The way you're shaking your left leg!
I was becoming a headliner in the South, but Colonel Tom Parker saw bigger things for me.
He promised me that if I signed him as my manager, I'd be a superstar.
Television! Movies! Son, there won't be a person in the country who doesn't know who Elvis Presley is!

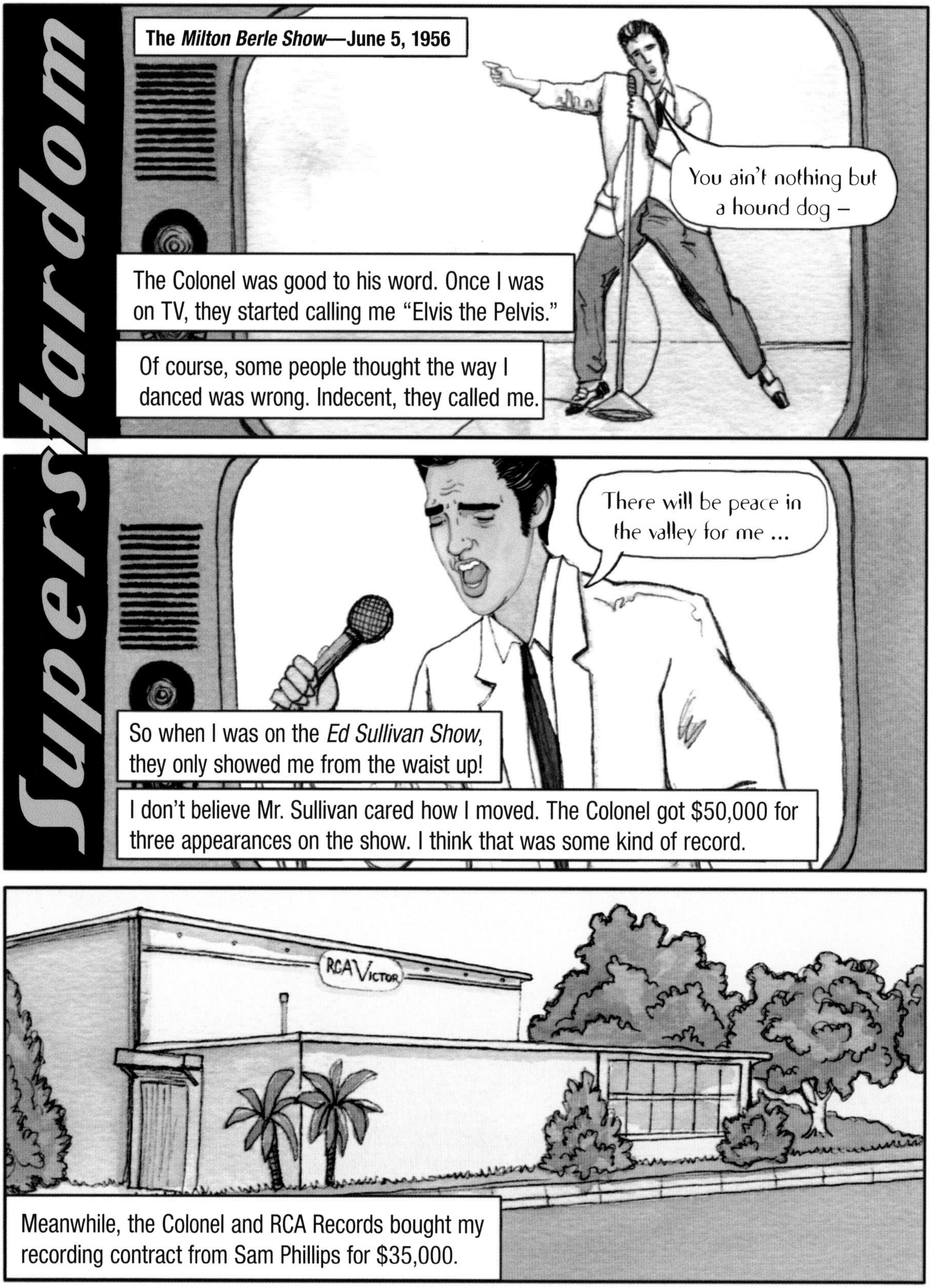
Superstardom
The Milton Berle Show—June 5, 1956
You ain't nothing but a hound dog –
The Colonel was good to his word. Once I was on TV, they started calling me "Elvis the Pelvis."
Of course, some people thought the way I danced was wrong. Indecent, they called me.
There will be peace in the valley for me ...
So when I was on the Ed Sullivan Show, they only showed me from the waist up!
I don't believe Mr. Sullivan cared how I moved. The Colonel got $50,000 for three appearances on the show. I think that was some kind of record.
RCA Victor
Meanwhile, the Colonel and RCA Records bought my recording contract from Sam Phillips for $35,000.

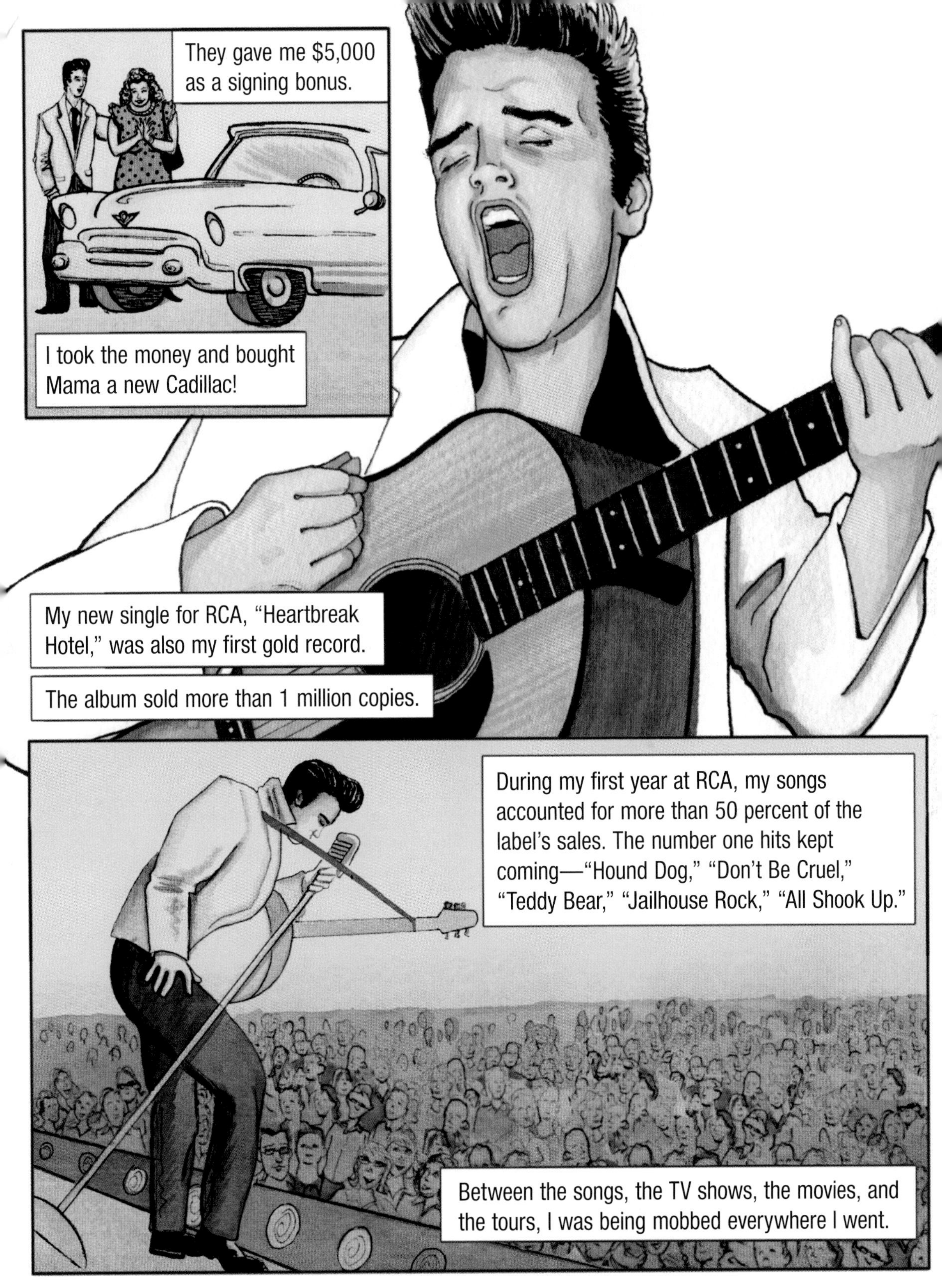
They gave me $5,000 as a signing bonus.
I took the money and bought Mama a new Cadillac!
My new single for RCA, "Heartbreak Hotel," was also my first gold record.
The album sold more than 1 million copies.
During my first year at RCA, my songs accounted for more than 50 percent of the label's sales. The number one hits kept coming—"Hound Dog," "Don't Be Cruel," "Teddy Bear," "Jailhouse Rock," "All Shook Up."
Between the songs, the TV shows, the movies, and the tours, I was being mobbed everywhere I went.

Private Elvis

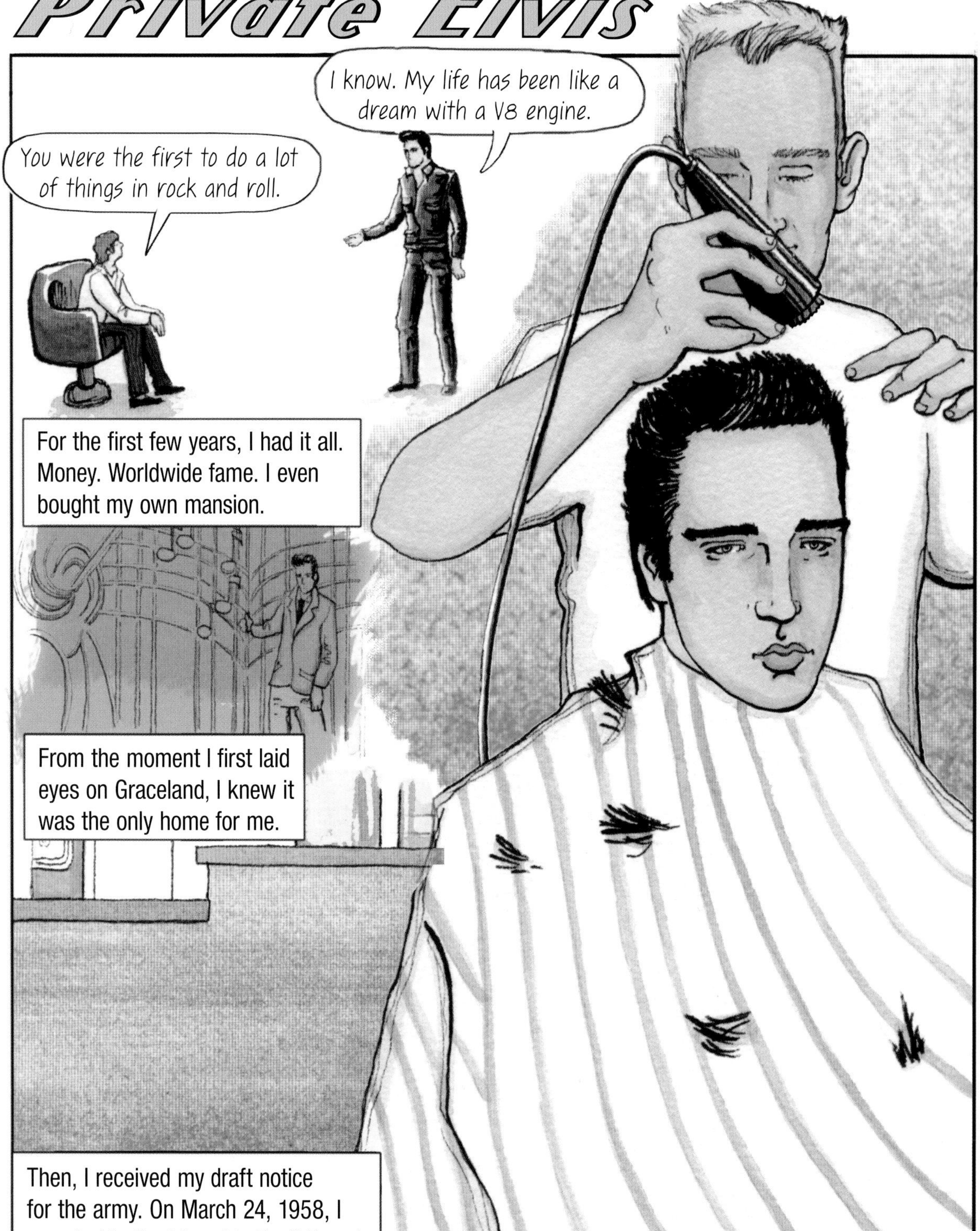
You were the first to do a lot of things in rock and roll.
I know. My life has been like a dream with a V8 engine.
For the first few years, I had it all. Money. Worldwide fame. I even bought my own mansion.
From the moment I first laid eyes on Graceland, I knew it was the only home for me.
Then, I received my draft notice for the army. On March 24, 1958, I reported to the Memphis Draft Board.

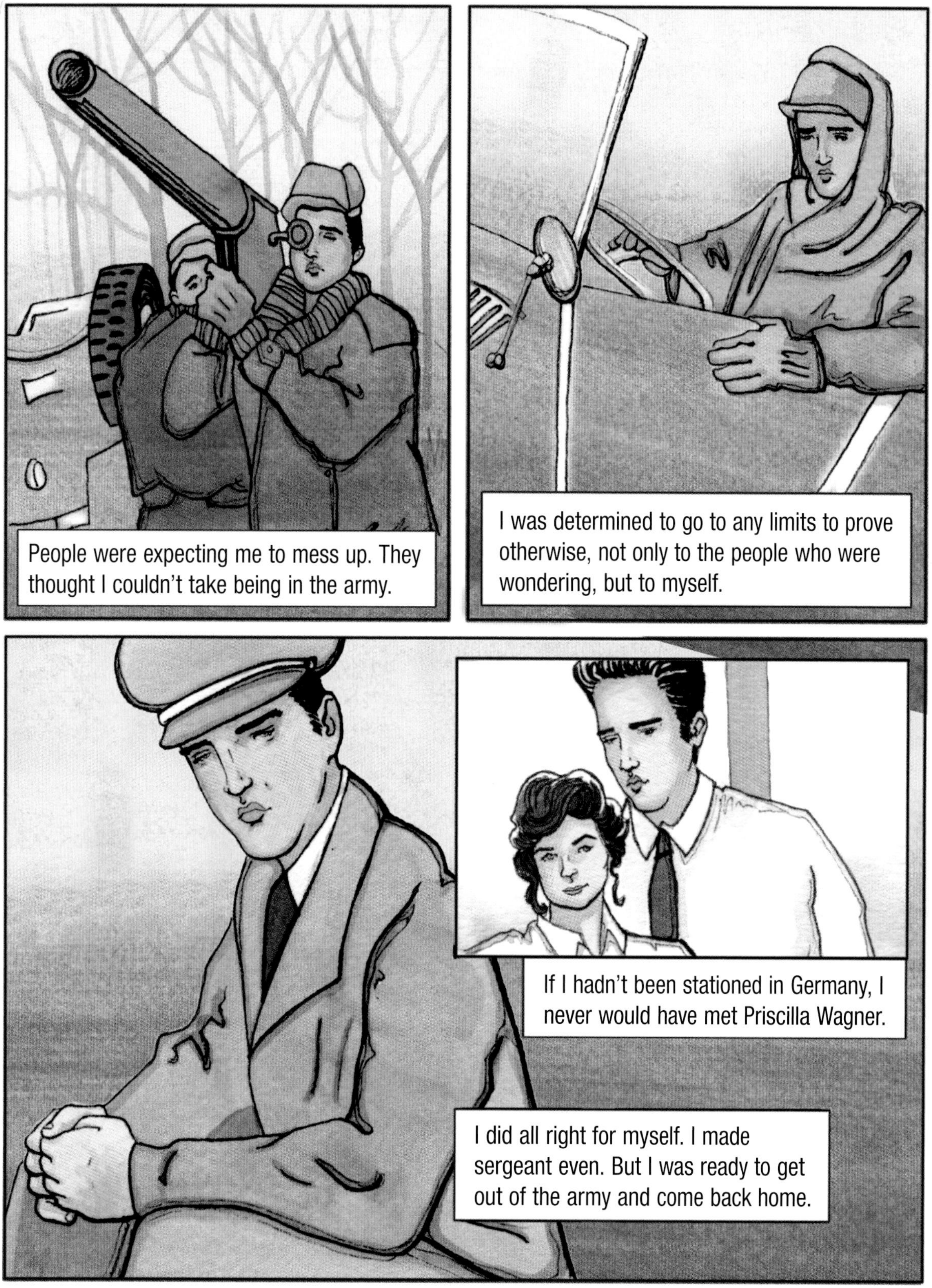
People were expecting me to mess up. They thought I couldn't take being in the army.
I was determined to go to any limits to prove otherwise, not only to the people who were wondering, but to myself.
If I hadn't been stationed in Germany, I never would have met Priscilla Wagner.
I did all right for myself. I made sergeant even. But I was ready to get out of the army and come back home.

Mr. and Mrs. Elvis Presley

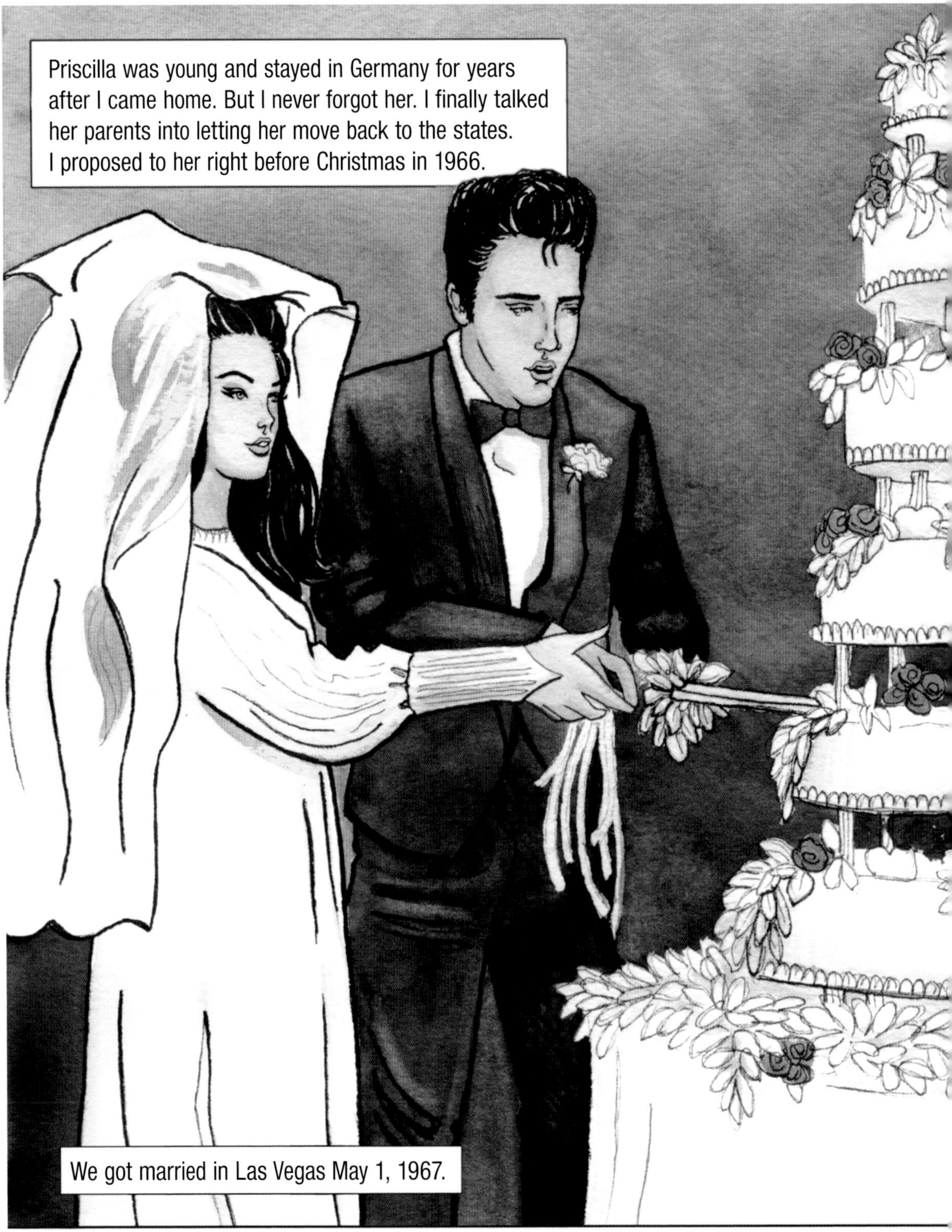
Priscilla was young and stayed in Germany for years after I came home. But I never forgot her. I finally talked her parents into letting her move back to the states. I proposed to her right before Christmas in 1966.
We got married in Las Vegas May 1, 1967.

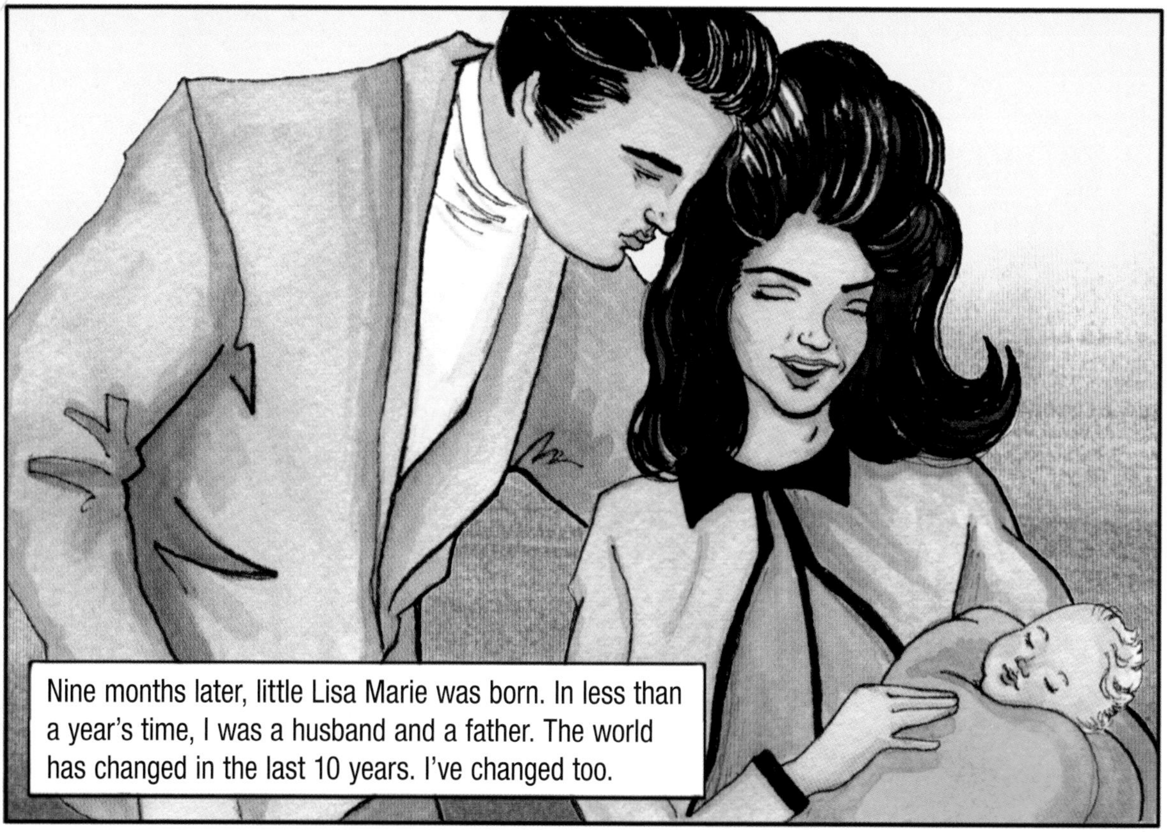

Nine months later, little Lisa Marie was born. In less than a year's time, I was a husband and a father. The world has changed in the last 10 years. I've changed too.

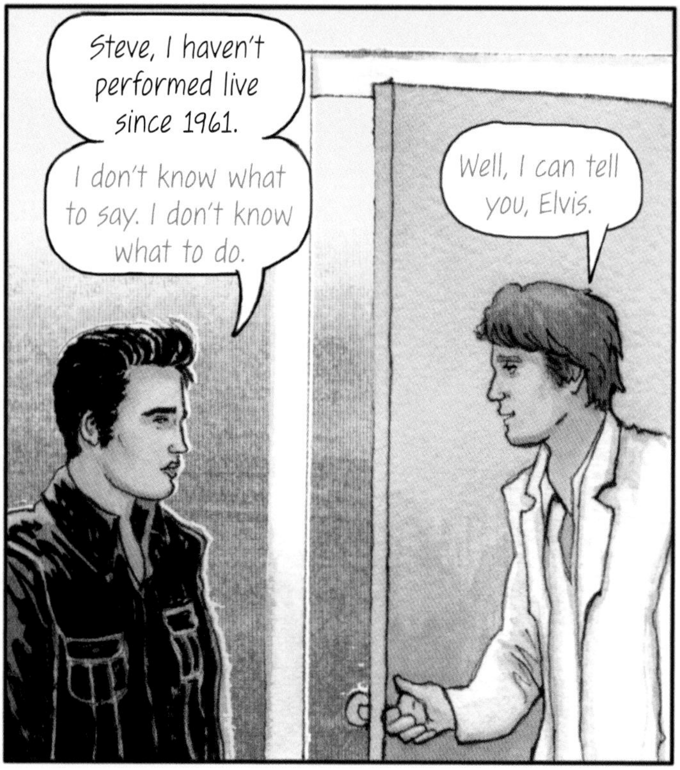

Steve, I haven't performed live since 1961.
I don't know what to say. I don't know what to do.
Well, I can tell you, Elvis.

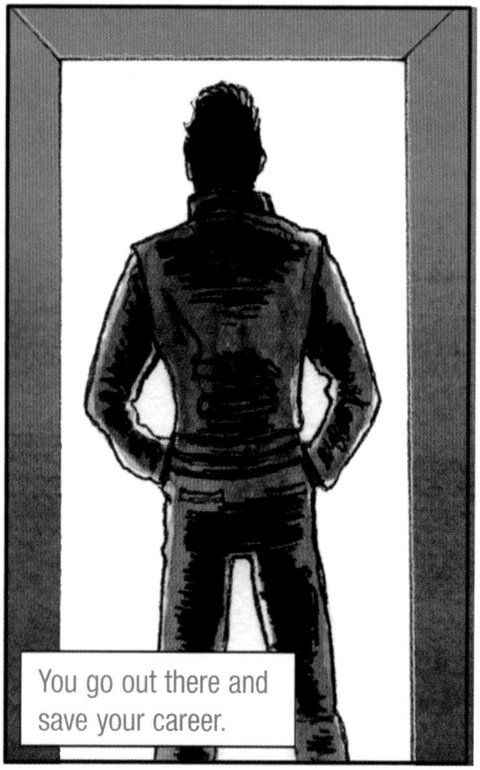

You go out there and save your career.

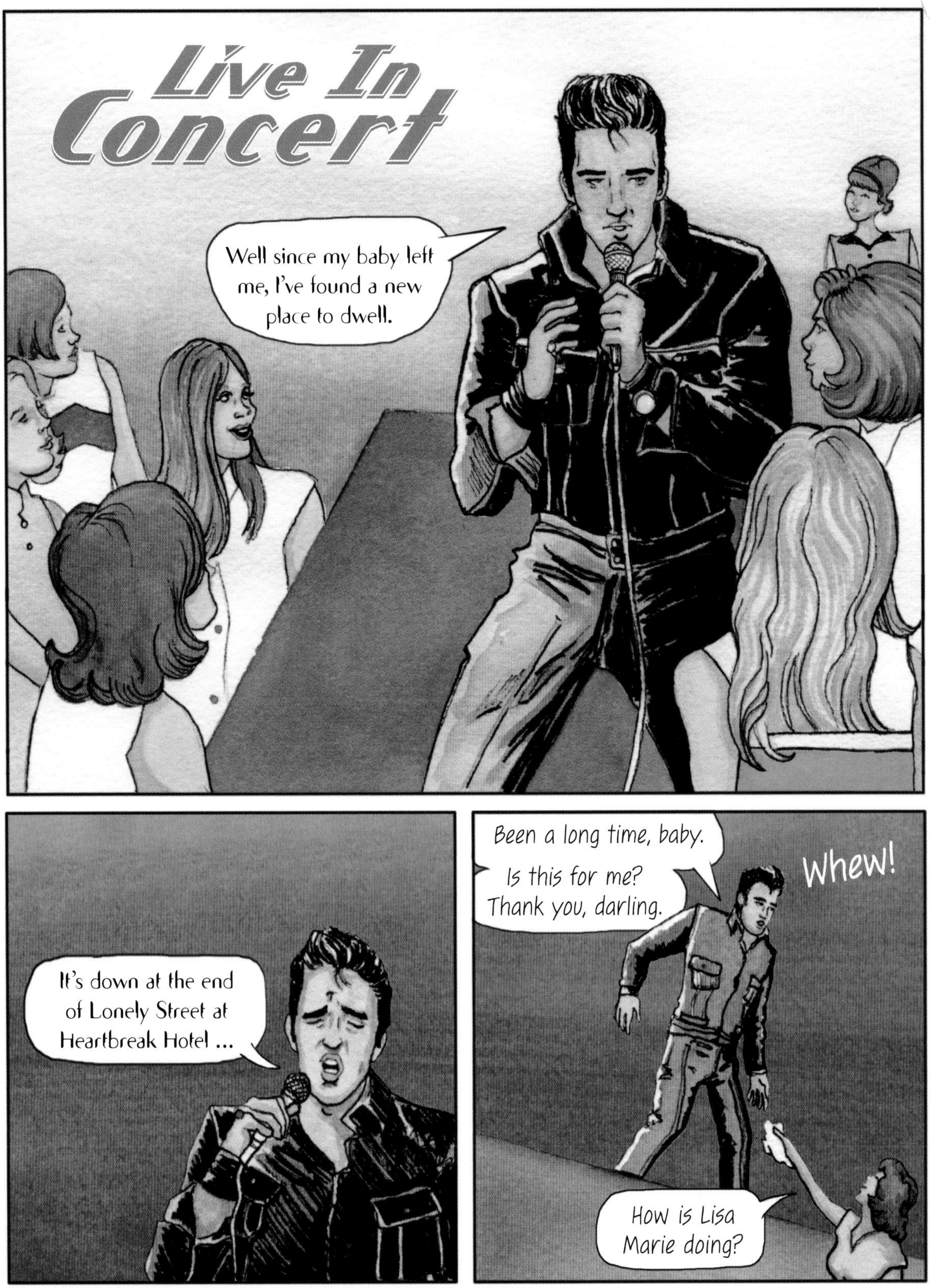
Live In Concert
Well since my baby left me, I've found a new place to dwell.
It's down at the end of Lonely Street at Heartbreak Hotel ...
Been a long time, baby.
Is this for me? Thank you, darling.
Whew!
How is Lisa Marie doing?

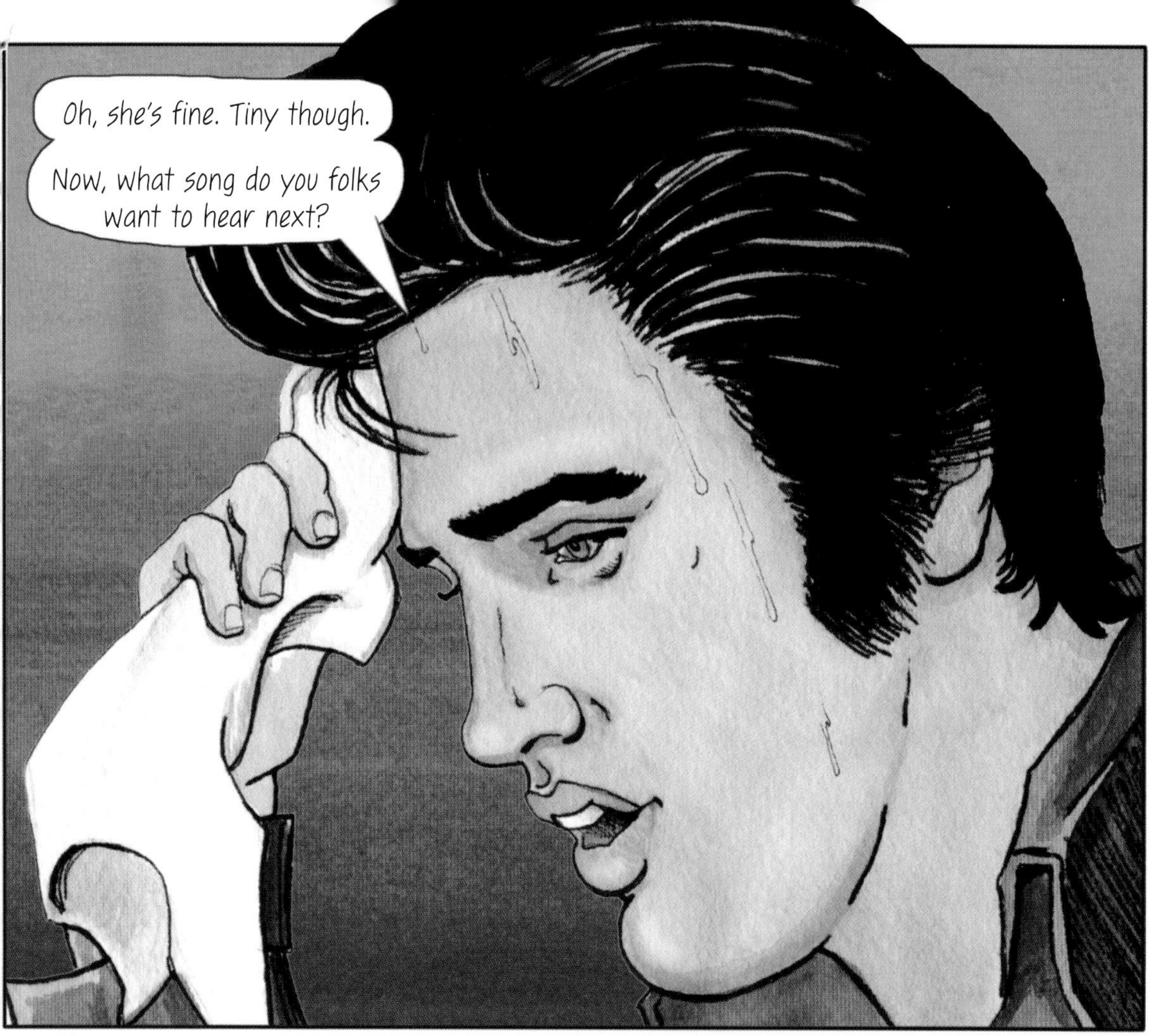
Oh, she's fine. Tiny though.
Now, what song do you folks want to hear next?

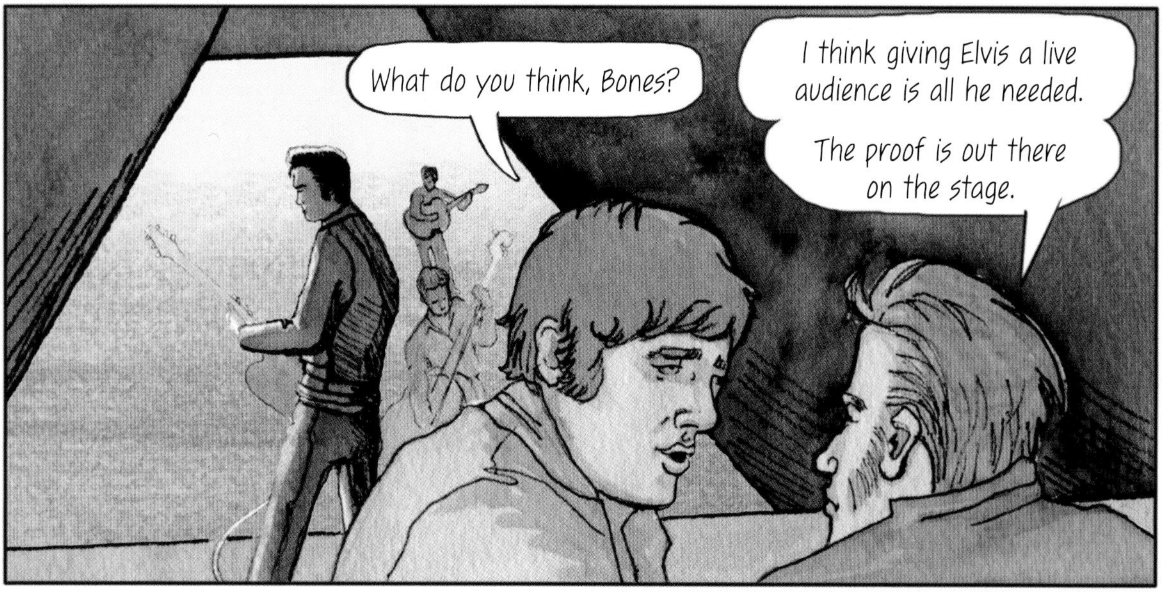
What do you think, Bones?
I think giving Elvis a live audience is all he needed.
The proof is out there on the stage.

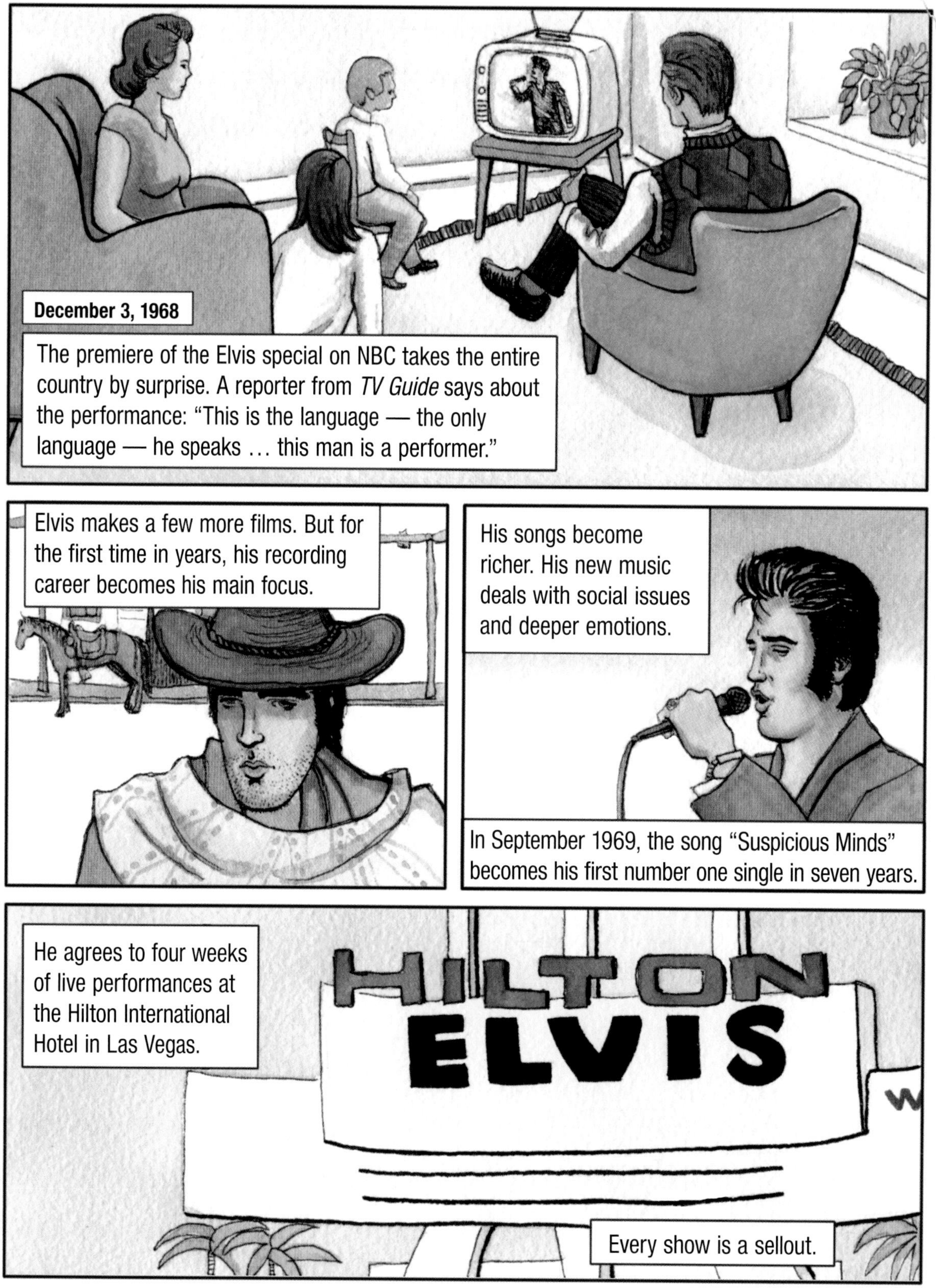
December 3, 1968
The premiere of the Elvis special on NBC takes the entire country by surprise. A reporter from *TV Guide* says about the performance: "This is the language — the only language — he speaks … this man is a performer."
Elvis makes a few more films. But for the first time in years, his recording career becomes his main focus.
His songs become richer. His new music deals with social issues and deeper emotions.
In September 1969, the song "Suspicious Minds" becomes his first number one single in seven years.
He agrees to four weeks of live performances at the Hilton International Hotel in Las Vegas.
HILTON
ELVIS
Every show is a sellout.

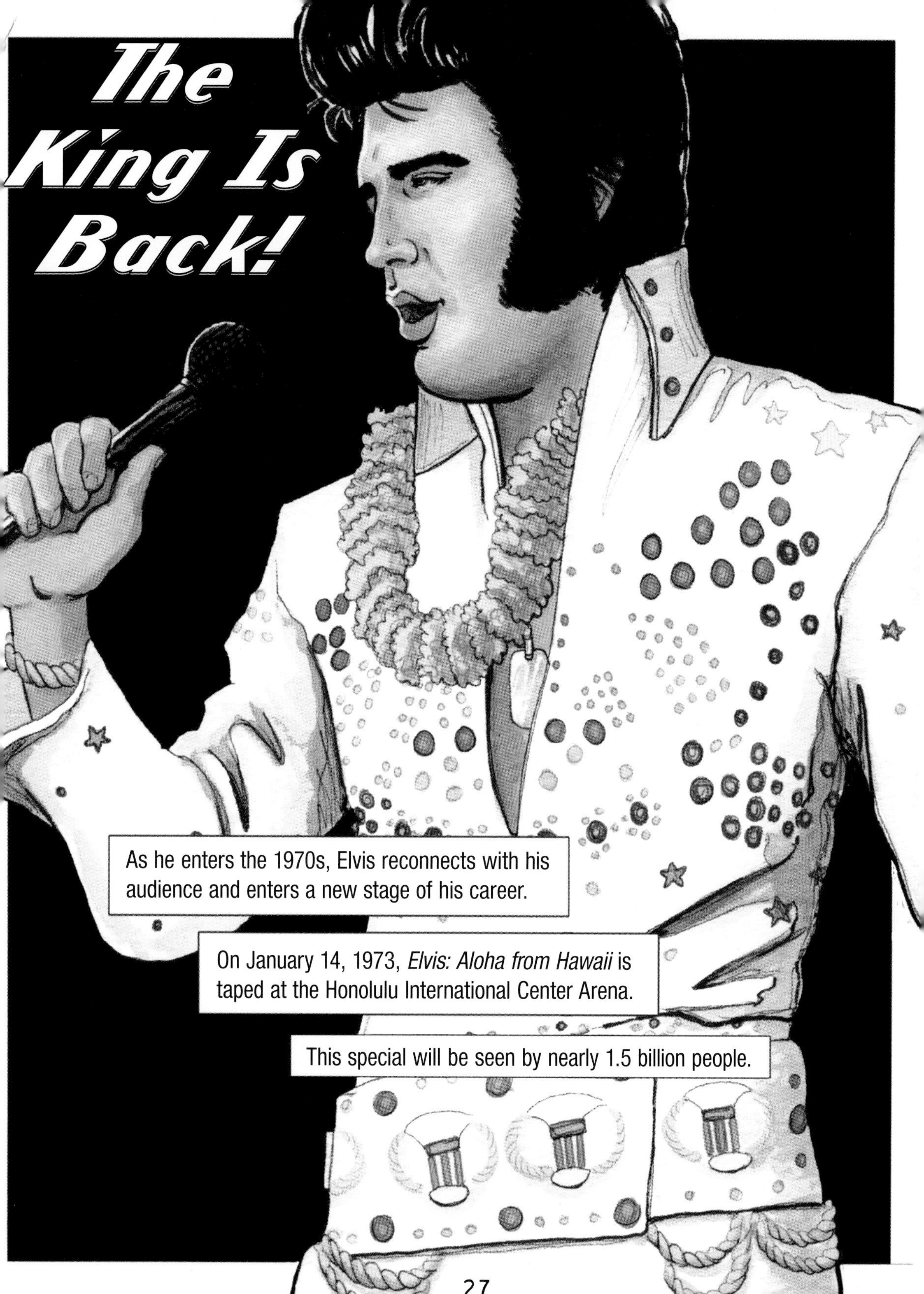

The King Is Back!
As he enters the 1970s, Elvis reconnects with his audience and enters a new stage of his career.
On January 14, 1973, *Elvis: Aloha from Hawaii* is taped at the Honolulu International Center Arena.
This special will be seen by nearly 1.5 billion people.

THE LEGACY OF ELVIS

Elvis Aaron Presley was born in East Tupelo, Mississippi, Tuesday, January 8, 1935. His twin brother, Jesse Garon, was stillborn. His parents, Vernon and Gladys Presley, adored their only child. Despite being poor, they worked to give Elvis a happy childhood. While close to his father, Elvis had an even stronger bond with his mother. She encouraged his dreams of becoming a singer.

In September 1948 the Presley family moved to Memphis, Tennessee, where Elvis attended Humes High School. After graduation, he worked as a truck driver for Crown Electric until his discovery by Sam Phillips. Phillips signed Elvis to Sun Records. A series of regional hits followed, along with several tours of the southeast. Then Colonel Tom Parker took over as Elvis' manager on August 18, 1955.

Parker ushered Elvis to RCA Records, where his first million-selling record, "Heartbreak Hotel" was released. In 1956 *Love Me Tender*, the first of Elvis' 33 movies, premiered to box office success. His rise to fame was temporarily halted when he was drafted into the U.S. Army. Before going overseas, tragedy struck. Elvis' mother, Gladys, died on August 14, 1958.

Upon returning from the armed forces in 1960, Elvis resumed his movie and recording career. As the decade continued, Elvis became less of a presence in the music industry. His 1968 television special for NBC was seen as a return to his roots as a singer.

Elvis returned to performing live. He also made a series of best-selling records until his sudden death on August 16, 1977, at age 42. His death stunned the world. Today, Elvis has sold more than 1 billion records, more than any other recording artist.

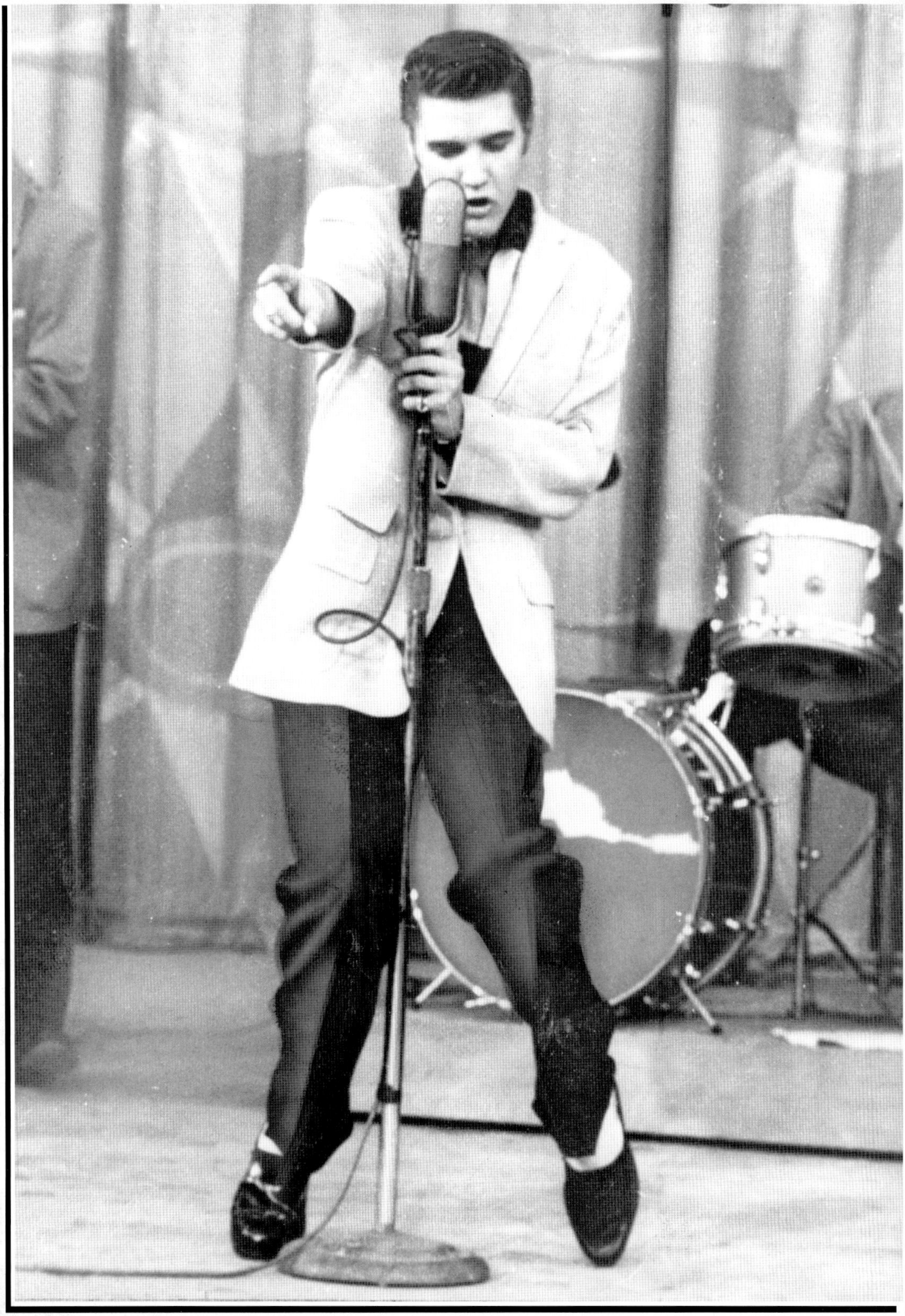

Glossary

album (AL-buhm)—a collection of music recorded on a CD, tape, or record

budget (BUHJ-it)—a plan for spending money

draft (DRAFT)—the selection of young men to serve in the army

duet (doo-ET)—a piece of music that is played or a song that is sung by two people

gospel (GOSS-puhl)—a religious style of music and singing

headliner (HED-line-uhr)—the main performer in a show

indecent (in-DEE-suhnt)—unpleasant, rude, or shocking

pelvis (PEL-viss)—the large bony structure near the base of the spine where the legs attach

producer (pruh-DOOSS-uhr)—a person in charge of putting on a play or making a movie or TV program

sergeant (SAR-juhnt)—an officer in the army or Marine Corps who is appointed from among the enlisted personnel

single (SING-guhl)—a recording with one song on each side

stationed (STAY-shuhnd)—to be assigned or set in a post or position

stillborn (STIL-born)—dead at birth

tour (TOOR)—when a band travels to different places to perform

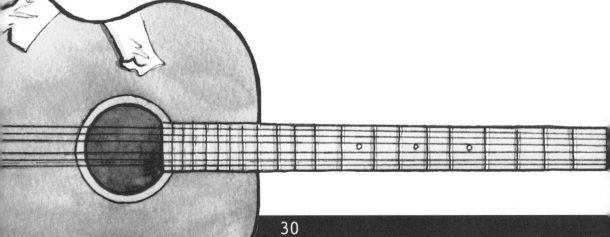

Read More

Doll, Susan. *Elvis Presley: With Profiles of Muddy Waters and Mick Jagger.* Biographical Connections. Chicago: World Book, 2007.

Edgers, Geoff. *Who Was Elvis Presley?* Who Was...? New York: Grosset & Dunlap, 2007.

Stewart, Mark. *Music Legends.* The Ultimate 10: Entertainment. Pleasantville, N.Y.: Gareth Stevens Pub., 2010.

Internet Sites

FactHound offers a safe, fun way to find Internet sites related to this book. All of the sites on FactHound have been researched by our staff.

Here's all you do:

Visit *www.facthound.com*

Type in this code: 9781429654760

Check out projects, games and lots more at
www.capstonekids.com

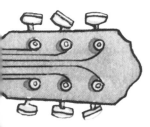

AMERICAN 🇺🇸 GRAPHIC